Praise for *Come Thirsty*

"Max strikes again! This time his message bathes the soul like a long awaited summer rain. Ahh…"

> — Bill Hybels
> Senior Pastor,
> Willow Creek Community Church

"One thing's for sure, people are *thirsty* for more than this world is ladling out. God bless my friend, Max, for leading a parched people to the well of Living Water. He shows us Jesus is the only one who can refresh us!"

> — Joni Eareckson Tada
> Founder and CEO, Joni and Friends

"In inimitable fashion, my friend Max demonstrates that as physical life is impossible apart from the unique composition of water, so spiritual life is inconceivable apart from the empowerment of 'living water.' He echoes the words of the Spirit and the bride, 'Whoever is thirsty, let him come; and whoever wishes let him take the free gift of the water of life.'"

> — Hank Hanegraaff
> Host of the *Bible Answer Man*
> Broadcast

"In *Come Thirsty* Max again does what he does best—he encourages us to dig deep into God's W-E-L-L, enabling and empowering us to experience the abundant life God desires for us."

> — John C. Maxwell
> Founder, The INJOY Group

"Max Lucado's insight and spiritual guidance have long been a source of strength, peace, and wisdom in my life. *Come Thirsty* is another light post along the road of my daily walk in the glory of Christ and a comforting reminder of how blessed we are to serve a Lord with an unlimited and refreshing reservoir of love, mercy, and grace."

> — Don Evans
> Secretary of Commerce

"Max Lucado has a way of touching a reader's heart through communicating the elements of the Gospel in a simple yet profound way. My prayer is that as you dip into the fountain of God's Holy Word, you will experience the satisfaction Max describes in the pages of *Come Thirsty*, and that your thirst will be quenched by the very Giver of the Water of Life."

> — Franklin Graham
> President & CEO, Samaritan's Purse
> and Billy Graham Evangelistic
> Association

"*Come Thirsty* is one of these books that will make the parched souls of its readers engulf each word with a refreshing enthusiasm. You may 'come thirsty,' but you will not leave disappointed. Drink deep my friends, this book is a gusher!"

— Bishop T.D. Jakes
Senior Pastor, The Potter's House

"Max Lucado's remarkable way with words makes us long to drink deeply from his well of knowledge and understanding. Amazingly, *Come Thirsty* both quenched my thirst and made me thirsty. Max helps us know we can never get enough of Him but what He gives is always enough."

— Mary Graham
President, Women of Faith

"Max Lucado weaves wonderful words that not only show you how to soothe your dehydrated heart, but how to do it daily and often. *Come Thirsty* is an ice-cold pick-me-up for a scorched spirit—a pitcher of pure grace for a dried-out soul."

— Dr. Tim Kimmel
Author of *Grace-Based Parenting*

"In *Come Thirsty*, Max reminds us that to live is more than to just survive; to seek what is eternal, not just temporary; and that God's love will satisfy our deepest needs, if we will simply receive it and drink it up."

— Senator John Cornyn

"Reading this book is like being on a long hard run, discovering a waterfall, and standing in it head tilted back, mouth open, arms open wide, receiving all its glorious refreshment. Those who 'come thirsty' are going to find themselves winsomely drawn to biblical truths as only Max can express them."

— Kay Arthur
Author and Co-CEO,
Precept Ministries International

"Who but Max Lucado could so beautifully walk us through the attributes of a thirst-quenching God? His stories at the start of each chapter are among his best ever and his ability to enrich our spiritual walk is unmatched. Those who 'come thirsty' to this book, will joyfully drink their fill."

— Kathy Troccoli
Singer and Author

"Like an oasis in the desert, *Come Thirsty* revitalizes even the weariest of spiritual travelers. Max Lucado has provided our parched generation with the roadmap to the everlasting well."

— Bob Russell, Senior Minister,
Southeast Christian Church,
Louisville, Kentucky

COME
THIRSTY

COME THIRSTY

MAX LUCADO

W PUBLISHING GROUP

A Division of Thomas Nelson Publishers

Since 1798

www.wpublishinggroup.com

Published by W Publishing Group, a Division of Thomas Nelson, Inc., P.O. Box 141000, Nashville, Tennessee 37214.

All Scripture quotations, unless otherwise indicated, are taken from The Holy Bible, New Living Translation, copyright © 1996. Used by permission of Tyndale House Publishers, Inc., Wheaton, Illinois 60189. All rights reserved. Other Scripture references are from the following sources: The Amplified Bible (AMP). Old Testament, copyright © 1965, 1987 by the Zondervan Corporation. The Amplified New Testament, copyright © 1954, 1958, 1987 by the Lockman Foundation. The Contemporary English Version (CEV) © 1991 by the American Bible Society. Used by permission. The Holy Bible, English Standard Version (ESV), copyright © 2001 by Crossway Bibles, a division of Good News Publishers. Used by permission. All rights reserved. The Good News Bible: The Bible in Today's English Version (TEV) © 1976, 1992 by the American Bible Society. The King James Version of the Bible (KJV). The Living Bible (TLB), copyright © 1971 by Tyndale House Publishers, Wheaton, Ill. Used by permission. The Message (MSG), copyright © 1993. Used by permission of NavPress Publishing Group. New American Standard Bible (NASB), © 1960, 1977, 1995 by the Lockman Foundation. The New Century Version® (NCV). Copyright © 1987, 1988, 1991 by Thomas Nelson, Inc. All rights reserved. The New English Bible (NEB) Copyright © 1961, 1970 by the Delegates of the Oxford University Press and the Syndics of the Cambridge University Press. The Holy Bible, New International Version (NIV). Copyright © 1973, 1978, 1984, International Bible Society. Used by permission of Zondervan Bible Publishers. The New King James Version (NKJV®), copyright 1979, 1980, 1982, Thomas Nelson, Inc., Publishers. J. B. Phillips: The New Testament in Modern English, Revised Edition (PHILLIPS). Copyright © J. B. Phillips 1958, 1960, 1972. Used by permission of Macmillan Publishing Co., Inc.

Library of Congress Cataloging-in-Publication Data

Lucado, Max.
    Come thirsty / by Max Lucado.
      p. cm.
    Includes bibliographical references.
    ISBN 0-8499-1761-1
    ISBN 0-8499-9130-7 (International Edition)
    1. Christian life. I. Title.
BV4501.3.L812 2004
248.4—dc22   2004007737

Printed in the United States of America

04 05 06 07 QW 9 8 7 6 5 4

ANDREA,

*your mom and I proudly dedicate this book to you
on your eighteenth birthday.*

Tell me, where have the years gone?

*If I knew, I'd gladly reclaim and relive each one of them.
We love you, dear daughter.*

May your smile never fade and your faith ever deepen.

Other Books by Max Lucado

INSPIRATIONAL

A Gentle Thunder
A Love Worth Giving
And the Angels Were Silent
God Came Near
He Chose the Nails
He Still Moves Stones
In the Eye of the Storm
In the Grip of Grace
It's Not About Me
Just Like Jesus
Next Door Savior
No Wonder They Call Him the Savior
On the Anvil
Six Hours One Friday
The Great House of God
Traveling Light
The Applause of Heaven
When Christ Comes
When God Whispers Your Name

CHILDREN'S BOOKS

Alabaster's Song
All You Ever Need
Because I Love You
He Chose You
Flo the Lyin' Fly
Hermie, A Common Caterpillar
If Only I Had a Green Nose
Jacob's Gift
Just in Case You Ever Wonder
Just the Way You Are
Just Like Jesus (for teens)

Contents

Part One
Accept His Work

Part Two
Rely on His Energy

Part Three
Trust His Lordship

Part Four
Receive His Love

Foreword

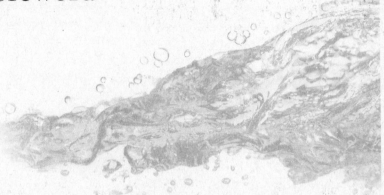

We all know what it is like to be thirsty—both physically and spiritually. That longing to quench your dry mouth can be powerful. But a dry heart—that's unbearable. You need refreshment, and you need it now. If your heart has become a little crusty, if your spirit is dry, if your heart is parched, you've come to the right place. In the pages of this book, Max leads us to the *w-e-l-l* that God provides for us. And, just as importantly, Max shows us how to receive from God *all* that He longs to give us.

It is often difficult for us to receive. But Max helps us grasp that, more than anything, God wants us to receive, to come thirsty and drink deeply from the living water available to each of us.

I have learned so much from Max Lucado. For years his books have been a consistent source of inspiration to me. And his friendship is something that I will always treasure. I have had the privilege of being ministered to one-on-one by Max, and I have had the wonderful opportunity to watch as he ministers—just as effectively—to an arena of fifteen thousand people.

My prayer for you, the reader, is that your soul is ministered to and refreshed through this wonderful book.

— Michael W. Smith

Acknowledgments

They prodded, applauded, extolled, and cajoled. These friends made the book a book. And to them I offer great gratitude.

Jim Barker—the God-seeking golf professional. You sowed these seeds while trying to fix my swing. At least the seeds bore fruit.

Liz Heaney and Karen Hill—If dentists had your skill, we'd have wider smiles and less pain. Great editing!

Carol Bartley—You did it again. We applaud your patient addiction to detail and precision.

Thanks to Hank Hanegraaff for generously giving your time and your insights.

David Moberg and W Publishing—You make me feel like a middle-schooler playing on an NBA squad!

The Oak Hills leadership and church family—celebrating our greatest year yet!

Susan Perry—Look up the word *servant* in the dictionary and see your picture. For your gracious service, thank you.

Jennifer McKinney—We appreciate your service almost as much as your smile.

Margaret Mechinus—Your skill at organization matches my proclivity toward chaos. Thanks for ensuring that at least my bookshelves make sense.

Charles Prince—true sage and dear friend. Thanks for the research.

Steve Halliday—Thanks to you, readers once again have another great discussion guide.

Andrew Cooley and the UpWords staff—a home-run-hitting team!

Steve and Cheryl Green—Denalyn and I regard you as permanent partners and dearest friends.

Michael W. Smith—Here's to many great moments together, and we're just getting started.

Jenna, Andrea, and Sara—The galaxy is missing three stars. Thanks to you, the whole world is brighter, especially mine.

My wife, Denalyn—Who would give a Renoir to a hillbilly? The Hope diamond to a pawnshop? Entrust a Lamborghini to a ten-year-old? I guess God would. For he gave you to me. And I'm still amazed.

And God—For your endless aquifer of grace, I thank you.

If you are thirsty, come!
If you want life-giving water,
come and take it.
It's free!

—Rev. 22:17 cev

Each of us is now a part of his resurrection body,
refreshed and sustained at one fountain—
his Spirit—where we all come to drink.

—I Cor. 12:13 msg

Meagan

Bentley Bishop stepped out of the elevator into a buzz of activity, all directed at him. The first voice was the urgent one of Eric, his producer.

"Mr. Bishop, I've been trying to reach you for the last two hours." Eric simmered with nervous energy. He stood a couple of inches over five feet in a wrinkled suit, loose tie, and the same scuffed loafers he'd worn for the last year. Though he was barely thirty, his hairline had retreated halfway and appeared on pace to soon evacuate the dome. His fashion turned no heads. But his media savvy did.

Eric read society like a radar screen. Departing fads, incoming trends, who teens followed, what executives ate—Eric knew the culture. As a result, he knew talk shows. He knew the hot topics, the best guests, and Bentley Bishop knew his show was in good hands with Eric. Even if he was prone to panic.

"I never carry a phone on the golf course, Eric. You know that."

"Didn't the pro shop tell you I'd called?"

"They did." By now the makeup artist was tying a bib around Bishop's neck. "Did I get some sun today, honey?" he asked, sizing her up with a head-to-toe look. She was young enough to be his daughter, but his glance wasn't paternal. "Then again, the red face may be your fault, Meagan. Seeing you always makes me blush."

Bishop's flirting repulsed everyone but Bishop. The production crew had seen him do the same with a dozen other girls. The two receptionists cut their eyes at each other. He used to sweet-talk them. Now he toyed with the "sweet thing in the tight jeans," or so they had heard him describe her.

Eric would fire Meagan in a heartbeat, but didn't have the authority. Meagan would leave in half a heartbeat, but needed the money.

"Mr. Bishop." Eric scowled, looking at his watch. "We've got a problem."

From down the hall came the announcement. "Fifteen minutes to air."

"Oops." Bishop winked, untying the makeup bib. "Looks like we'll have to finish this later, babe."

Meagan powdered his cheek one final time and forced a smile.

"Dr. Allsup canceled," Eric inserted as the two headed for the studio.

"What?"

"Weather. He called from O'Hare."

"The Midwest is having weather problems?"

"Apparently Chicago is."

The two stopped in the middle of the hallway, and for the first time, Bishop gave Eric his full attention. He loomed over his producer by a full foot, his mane of thick white hair making him look even taller. Everyone in America, it seemed, recognized that square

jaw and those caterpillar eyebrows. Twenty years of nightly inter-
views had elevated him to billboard status.

"What's our topic?" he asked.

"Surviving stress."

"Appropriate. Did you phone some fill-ins?"

"I did."

"Dr. Varner?"

"Sick."

"Dr. Chambers?"

"Out of town."

"What about those two guys we had last month who wrote that
breathing book?"

"*Breathe Right, Live Right.* One has a cold. The other didn't call
back."

"Then we're stuck with the rabbi."

"He's out too."

"Rabbi Cohen? He's never out. He's been subbing for ten years."

"Fifteen. His sister died and he's in Topeka."

"So where does that leave us? Doing a remote? I don't like
remotes." By now Bishop's voice was beginning to boom and Eric's
face to redden. The ninth-floor hallway of the Burbank Plaza
Building was silent—busy, but silent. No one envied Eric.

"No remote, Mr. Bishop. The system is down."

"What?"

"Lightning from last night's storm."

"Did we have a storm last night?" Bishop asked everyone in
hearing distance.

Eric shrugged. "I had us hooked up with the president's
physician, then discovered the technical problems. No outside
feeds."

The smile had long since vanished from Bishop's face. "No guests. No feeds. Why didn't you call me?"

Eric knew better than to answer honestly.

"Studio audience?"

"Packed. They came to see Dr. Allsup."

"So what do we do?" Bishop demanded.

"Ten minutes!" came a voice.

"We have a guest," Eric explained, slowly turning toward the studio door. "He's already in makeup."

"Where did you find him?"

"I think he found us." By now they were walking fast. "He sent me an e-mail an hour ago."

"How did he get your e-mail address?"

"I don't know. Nor do I know how he found out about our situation, but he did." Eric pulled a piece of paper from his jacket side pocket. "He told me he's sorry about Varner, Chambers, the Chicago weather, and last night's lightning. But he didn't like the breathing book anyway. And, knowing our plight, he volunteered to do the show."

"That's crazy." Eric opened the door. Bishop entered, never losing eye contact with Eric. "You let him in?"

"Actually, he sort of let himself in. But I called around. He's causing quite a stir, mainly in smaller markets. Teaches ethics at a junior college near Birmingham. Some religious leaders are concerned, but the rank and file like him. He lectures at colleges, popular on the banquet circuit. Talks a lot about finding peace in your soul."

By now Bishop was stepping toward the set. "I could use some peace. Hope this guy's good. What's his name?"

"Jesse. Jesse Carpenter."

"Never heard of him. Let's give him fifteen minutes. For the last half of the program, rerun the highlight show."

"But we did that last week."

"People forget. Go to makeup and check on this Carpenter fellow."

Meagan could see both her face and Jesse's in the mirror. She would later describe him as nice looking but not heart stopping. He wore a brown, elbow-patched corduroy coat, khaki slacks, and an acceptable but forgettable tie. A straight part separated his hair on the side, giving it a just-cut look. Meagan tied the apron around his neck and began with polite chitchat. His smile required no coaxing.

"First time on the show?"

"Yes."

"First time to the West Coast?"

"You might say that."

Meagan dabbed base powder on his cheeks, then stopped. He was staring at her. "Is this required?" he asked. He wasn't enjoying the drill.

"Keeps the glare down," she explained.

As she powdered, Jesse closed his eyes, then opened them and looked at her, saying nothing.

Meagan wondered about him. When men stared at her, she knew what they wanted. He's probably the same. She stepped behind the chair and sprayed his hair. He closed his eyes again. She looked at herself, curious what he might think of her—tattooed rose on her neck, jet-black hair and fingernails. T-shirt tied tight in the back, leaving her stomach exposed. A far cry from her role as a majorette in the high-school band. Her older brother, who managed the family pharmacy in Missouri, was always calling and asking, "You're not getting a tattoo, are you? And keep those rings out of your nose." She didn't listen.

She really didn't care what he thought. After all, she was twenty-one. Can't a girl have a life?

"Architecture?"

The one-word question caught Meagan off guard. "What?"

Jesse had opened his eyes, and with them he gestured to her open backpack that sat on the counter. A copy of *Architectural Digest* leaned out.

"Call it a secret interest," she explained. "Who knows, someday . . ."

"Have any other secrets?"

Meagan sighed. Of all the come-ons. "None that you need to hear about." She shrugged.

Men never ceased to amaze her. Her mother's warning was right: no matter how nice they look, first the line, then the hook. For a couple of minutes neither spoke. Meagan liked it that way. She found safety in silence. Jesse, however, wasn't finished.

"Bishop asks a lot of you."

Meagan cocked her head. "Is that a question?"

"No, just the truth."

"He's all right." Meagan sidestepped the topic, intentionally avoiding Jesse's eyes as she dusted his forehead one last time.

Jesse's tone was solemn. "Meagan, don't let your heart get hard. You were not made to be this edgy, this crusty."

She dropped her hands to her side and looked at Jesse, at first offended, then curious.

"What do you know about me?"

"I know you are a better person than this. I also know it's not too late to make a change. This street you're traveling? The houses look nice, but the road goes nowhere."

She started to object, but his eyes caught hers. "I can help, Meagan. I really can."

"I don't need your help" were the words she started to say, but didn't. He smiled softly, reassuringly. More silence followed. Not awkward. Just silence. Meagan felt a smile forming in reply, but then . . .

"Five minutes!" shouted a studio voice. Meagan looked up to see Eric's face.

Meagan never watched the *Bentley Bishop Show*. The first couple of days she had tried but quickly grew weary of his piano-key smile and disc-jockey voice. So she lost interest. She tried chatting with other staff members, but they knew how she got and kept her job. Show veterans formed a tight club, and girls like Meagan needn't apply for membership. "You'd think I was a leper," she'd mumbled after her final attempt at conversation.

Meagan followed her daily ritual of cleaning her counter, pulling out her magazine, and sitting in the makeup chair. But on this day, as she lifted the remote to turn off the makeup-room monitor, she saw Jesse walk out on stage.

People offered polite applause. She watched Jesse greet the host, take his seat, and nod at the crowd. Bishop turned his attention to the index cards resting on the table, each bearing an Eric-prepared question. He gave them a shuffle and set things in motion.

"Tell us about yourself, Mr. Carpenter. I understand you teach at a community college."

"Night courses mainly."

"In Alabama?"

"Yessir. Sawgrass, Alabama."

"Do people in Sawgrass know the meaning of stress?"

Jesse nodded.

Bishop continued: "This is a tough, tough world, Jesse. Brutally competitive, highly demanding. Tell us, how do we handle the stress?"

The teacher sat up a bit straighter, made a tent with his hands, and began to speak. "Stress signals a deeper need, a longing. We long to fit in, to make a difference. Acceptance, significance—these matter to us. So we do what it takes; we go into debt to buy the house, we stretch the credit card to buy the clothes . . . and life on the treadmill begins."

"Treadmill?"

"Right, we spend a lot of energy going nowhere. At the end of the day, or the end of a life, we haven't moved one step. We're stuck."

"What do we do about it?"

"What we *typically* do doesn't work. We take vacations. We take pills. We take our chances in Vegas. We take advantage of younger women . . ." Jesse looked straight at Bishop as he spoke. But if Bishop connected the dots, he didn't show it.

Meagan did, and for the first time in a long time, she smiled.

"Doesn't work, Mr. Bishop. Back home we call it 'sipping out of the swamp.' There's stuff in that water we were never made to drink." This time Jesse turned toward the camera.

For a moment Meagan felt as if he were speaking to her, just to her. In self-defense, she muted the sound and watched him speak.

His minutes on the show totaled no more than seven. She later heard that Bishop and Eric were pleased, even interested in asking him to return.

She hoped they would.

※

Jesse spotted Meagan through the window of a café, squeezing lemon into her glass of water. For a couple of minutes he watched. The restaurant had a retro look, a throwback to diner days with soda counters and silver-rimmed tables. Two men in an adjacent booth said something to her; she ignored them. A server offered her a menu; she declined it. A car screeched to a stop and honked at a jaywalking pedestrian; she looked up. That's when Meagan saw him.

Jesse smiled. She didn't. But neither did she turn away. She watched him cross the narrow street, enter the café, and walk toward her booth. He asked if he could join her, and she nodded. As he signaled the server, Meagan noticed Jesse looked tired.

He said little as he waited on his coffee. She spoke even less, at first. But once she began, her whole story tumbled out. Dropped by a boyfriend in Missouri. Fed up with her family. Someone told her she could make fast money in commercials. Escaped to the West Coast. Audition after audition. Rejection after rejection. Finally cosmetics school. "I never even finished," she confessed. "I heard about the opening at Bentley Bishop's. Went for an interview and . . ."—she looked away—"after doing what he wanted, he hired me. And now"—a tear bubbled—"I'm here. I pay the rent and don't go hungry. Twenty-one years old and surviving L.A. Sounds like the chorus of a country-western song. But I'm okay. At least that's what I tell myself."

Jesse's sandwich arrived. He offered her half, but she declined. After a couple of bites, he wiped his mouth with a napkin.

"Meagan, I know you. I've watched you stain pillows with tears and walk streets because you couldn't sleep. I know you. And I know you hate who you are becoming."

"So"—Meagan touched the corner of her eye with the back of a knuckle—"if you're such a psychic, tell me: where's God in all this? I've been looking for him a long, long time." With a sudden increase in volume, she began listing misdeeds on her fingers. "I ran out on my folks. I sleep with my boss. I've spent more time on a barstool than a church pew. I'm tired, tired of it all." She bit her lip and looked away.

Jesse inclined the same direction and caught her attention. She looked up to see him beaming, energetic, as though he were an algebra professor and she was struggling with two plus two.

"Where is God in all this?" He repeated her question. "Nearer than you've ever dreamed." He took her glass and held it. "Meagan, everyone who drinks this water will get thirsty again. But I offer a different drink. Anyone who drinks the water I give will never thirst. Not ever."

Again, silence.

With a finger Meagan bounced the ice cubes in the glass. Finally she asked, "Never?"

"Not ever."

She looked away, then looked back, and, with every ounce of honesty she owned, asked, "Tell me, Jesse. Who in the world are you?"

Her new friend leaned forward in response and replied, "I thought you'd never ask."

ONE

The Dehydrated Heart

You're acquainted with physical thirst. Your body, according to some estimates, is 80 percent fluid. That means a man my size lugs around 160 pounds of water. Apart from brains, bones, and a few organs, we're walking water balloons.

We need to be. Stop drinking and see what happens. Coherent thoughts vanish, skin grows clammy, and vital organs wrinkle. Your eyes need fluid to cry; your mouth needs moisture to swallow; your glands need sweat to keep your body cool; your cells need blood to carry them; your joints need fluid to lubricate them. Your body needs water the same way a tire needs air.

In fact, your Maker wired you with thirst—a "low-fluid indicator." Let your fluid level grow low, and watch the signals flare. Dry mouth. Thick tongue. Achy head. Weak knees. Deprive your body of necessary fluid, and your body will tell you.

Deprive your soul of spiritual water, and your soul will tell you. Dehydrated hearts send desperate messages. Snarling tempers. Waves of worry. Growling mastodons of guilt and fear. You think

God wants you to live with these? Hopelessness. Sleeplessness. Loneliness. Resentment. Irritability. Insecurity. These are warnings. Symptoms of a dryness deep within.

Perhaps you've never seen them as such. You've thought they, like speed bumps, are a necessary part of the journey. Anxiety, you assume, runs in your genes like eye color. Some people have bad ankles; others, high cholesterol or receding hairlines. And you? You fret.

And moodiness? Everyone has gloomy days, sad Saturdays. Aren't such emotions inevitable? Absolutely. But unquenchable? No way. View the pains of your heart, not as struggles to endure, but as an inner thirst to slake—proof that something within you is starting to shrivel.

Treat your soul as you treat your thirst. Take a gulp. Imbibe moisture. Flood your heart with a good swallow of water.

Where do you find water for the soul? Jesus gave an answer one October day in Jerusalem. People had packed the streets for the annual reenactment of the rock-giving-water miracle of Moses. In honor of their nomadic ancestors, they slept in tents. In tribute to the desert stream, they poured out water. Each morning a priest filled a golden pitcher with water from the Gihon spring and carried it down a people-lined path to the temple. Announced by trumpets, the priest encircled the altar with a libation of liquid. He did this every day, once a day, for seven days. Then on the last day, the great day, the priest gave the altar a Jericho loop—seven circles—dousing it with seven vessels of water. It may have been at this very moment that the rustic rabbi from the northlands commanded the people's attention. "On the last day, that great day of the feast, Jesus stood and cried out, saying, 'If anyone thirsts, let him come to Me and drink. He who believes in Me, as the

Scripture has said, out of his heart will flow rivers of living water'" (John 7:37–38 NKJV).

Finely frocked priests turned. Surprised people looked. Wide-eyed children and toothless grandparents paused. They knew this man. Some had heard him preach in the Hebrew hills; others, in the city streets. Two and a half years had passed since he'd emerged from the Jordan waters. The crowd had seen this carpenter before.

But had they seen him this intense? He "stood and shouted" (NLT). The traditional rabbinic teaching posture was sitting and speaking. But Jesus stood up and shouted out. The blind man shouted, appealing for sight (Mark 10:46–47); the sinking Peter shouted, begging for help (Matt. 14:29–30); and the demon-possessed man shouted, pleading for mercy (Mark 5:2–7). John uses the same Greek verb to portray the volume of Jesus's voice. Forget a kind clearing of the throat. God was pounding his gavel on heaven's bench. Christ demanded attention.

He shouted because his time was short. The sand in the neck of his hourglass was down to measurable grains. In six months he'd be dragging a cross through these streets. And the people? The people thirsted. They needed water, not for their throats, but for their hearts. So Jesus invited: *Are your insides starting to shrivel? Drink me.*

What H_2O can do for your body, Jesus can do for your heart. Lubricate it. Aquify it. Soften what is crusty, flush what is rusty. How?

Like water, Jesus goes where we can't. Throw a person against a wall, his body thuds and drops. Splash water against a wall, and the liquid conforms and spreads. Its molecular makeup grants water great flexibility: one moment separating and seeping into a crack, another collecting and thundering over the Victoria Falls. Water goes where we cannot.

So does Jesus. He is a spirit and, although he forever has a body, he is not bound by a body. In fact, John parenthetically explains, "(When he said 'living water,' he was speaking of the Spirit, who would be given to everyone believing in him . . .)" (John 7:39). The Spirit of Jesus threads down the throat of your soul, flushing fears, dislodging regrets. He does for your soul what water does for your body. And, thankfully, we don't have to give him directions.

We give none to water, do we? Before swallowing, do you look at the liquid and say, "Ten drops of you go to my spleen. I need fifty on cardiovascular detail. The rest of you head north to my scalp. It's really itchy today." Water somehow knows where to go.

Jesus knows the same. Your directions are not needed, but your permission is. Like water, Jesus won't come in unless swallowed. That is, we must willingly surrender to his lordship. You can stand waist deep in the Colorado River and still die of thirst. Until you scoop and swallow, the water does your system no good. Until you gulp Christ, the same is true.

Don't you need a drink? Don't you long to flush out the fear, anxiety, and guilt? You can. Note the audience of his invitation. "If *anyone* thirsts, let him come to Me and drink" (v. 37 NKJV, emphasis mine). Are you *anyone?* If so, then step up to the well. You qualify for his water.

All ages are welcome. Both genders invited. No race excluded. Scoundrels. Scamps. Rascals and rubes. All welcome. You don't have to be rich to drink, religious to drink, successful to drink; you simply need to follow the instructions on what—or better, *who*—to drink. Him. In order for Jesus to do what water does, you must let him penetrate your heart. Deep, deep inside.

Internalize him. Ingest him. Welcome him into the inner workings of your life. Let Christ be the water of your soul.

How is this done? Begin by heeding your thirst. Don't dismiss your loneliness. Don't deny your anger. Your restless spirit, churning stomach, the sense of dread that turns your armpits into swamplands—these are signal flares exploding in the sky. *We could use a little moisture down here!* Don't let your heart shrink into a raisin. For the sake of those who need your love, hydrate your soul! Heed your thirst.

And drink good water. You don't gulp dirt or swallow rocks. Do you drink plastic or paper or pepper? Mercy no! When it comes to thirst of the body, we've learned how to reach for the right stuff. Do the same for your heart. Not everything you put to your lips will help your thirst. The arms of forbidden love may satisfy for a time, but only for a time. Eighty-hour workweeks grant a sense of fulfillment, but never remove the thirst.

Take special concern with the bottle labeled "religion." Jesus did. Note the setting in which he speaks. He isn't talking to prostitutes or troublemakers, penitentiary inmates or reform-school students. No, he addresses churchgoers at a religious convention. This day is an ecclesiastical highlight; like the Vatican on Easter Sunday. You half expect the pope to appear in the next verse. Religious symbols are laid out like a yard sale: the temple, the altar, trumpets, and robes. He could have pointed to any item as a source of drink. But he doesn't. These are mere symbols.

He points to himself, the one to whom the symbols point and in whom they are fulfilled. Religion pacifies, but never satisfies. Church activities might hide a thirst, but only Christ quenches it. Drink *him*.

And drink often. Jesus employs a verb that suggests repeated swallows. Literally, "Let him come to me and drink and keep drinking." One bottle won't satisfy your thirst. Regular sips satisfy thirsty throats. Ceaseless communion satisfies thirsty souls.

Toward this end, I give you this tool: a prayer for the thirsty heart. Carry it just as a cyclist carries a water bottle. The prayer outlines four essential fluids for soul hydration: God's work, God's energy, his lordship, and his love. You'll find the prayer easy to remember. Just think of the word W-E-L-L.

Lord, I come thirsty. I come to drink, to receive. I receive your *work* on the cross and in your resurrection. My sins are pardoned, and my death is defeated. I receive your *energy*. Empowered by your Holy Spirit, I can do all things through Christ, who gives me strength. I receive your *lordship*. I belong to you. Nothing comes to me that hasn't passed through you. And I receive your *love*. Nothing can separate me from your love.

Don't you need regular sips from God's reservoir? I do. I've offered this prayer in countless situations: stressful meetings, dull days, long drives, demanding trips, character-testing decisions. Many times a day I step to the underground spring of God and receive anew his work for my sin and death, the energy of his Spirit, his lordship, and his love.

Drink with me from his bottomless well. You don't have to live with a dehydrated heart.

Receive Christ's *work* on the cross,
    the *energy* of his Spirit,
        his *lordship* over your life,
            his unending, unfailing *love*.

Drink deeply and often. And out of you will flow rivers of living water.

Part One

Accept His
Work

TWO

Sin Vaccination

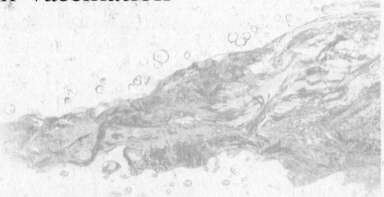

In October of 1347, a Genoese fleet returned from the Black Sea, carrying in its cargo the death sentence for Europe. By the time the ships landed in Messina, Italy, most of the sailors were dead. The few who survived wished they hadn't. Fever racked their bodies. Festering boils volcanoed on their skin. Authorities ordered the vessels out of the harbor, but it was too late. Flea-infested rats had already scampered down the ropes into the village, and the bubonic dictator had begun its ruthless march across the continent.

The disease followed trade routes northward through Italy into France and the northern nations. By spring it had breached the border of England. Within a short and brutal five years, twenty-five million people, one-third of Europe's population, had died. And that was just the beginning.

Three centuries later it still raged. As late as 1665 an epidemic left a hundred thousand Londoners dead, taking some seven thousand lives a week until a bitter, yet mercifully cold, winter killed the fleas.

No cure was known. No hope was offered. The healthy quarantined the infected. The infected counted their days.

When you make a list of history's harshest scourges, rank the Black Plague near the top. It earns a high spot. But not the highest. Call the disease catastrophic, disastrous. But humanity's deadliest? No. Scripture reserves that title for a darker blight, an older pandemic that by comparison makes the Black Plague seem like a cold sore. No culture avoids, no nation escapes, no person sidesteps the infection of sin.

Blame the bubonic plague on the *Yersinia pestis* bacterium. Blame the plague of sin on a godless decision. Adam and Eve turned their heads toward the hiss of the snake and for the first time ignored God. Eve did not ask, "God, what do you want?" Adam didn't suggest, "Let's consult the Creator." They acted as if they had no heavenly Father. His will was ignored, and sin, with death on its coattails, entered the world.

Sin sees the world with no God in it.

Where we might think of sin as slip-ups or missteps, God views sin as a godless attitude that leads to godless actions. "All of us have strayed away like sheep. We have left God's paths to follow our own" (Isa. 53:6). The sinful mind dismisses God. His counsel goes unconsulted. His opinion, unsolicited. His plan, unconsidered. The sin-infected grant God the same respect middle-schoolers give a substitute teacher—acknowledged, but not taken seriously.

The lack of God-centeredness leads to self-centeredness. Sin celebrates its middle letter—sIn. It proclaims, "It's your life, right? Pump your body with drugs, your mind with greed, your nights with pleasure." The godless lead a me-dominated, childish life, a life of "doing what we felt like doing, when we felt like doing it" (Eph. 2:3 MSG).

God says to love. I choose to hate.

God instructs, "Forgive." I opt to get even.

God calls for self-control. I promote self-indulgence.

Sin, for a season, quenches thirst. But so does salt water. Given time, the thirst returns, more demanding and demanding more than ever. "Having lost all sensitivity, they have given themselves over to sensuality so as to indulge in every kind of impurity, with a *continual lust for more*" (Eph. 4:19 NIV, emphasis mine).

We pay a high price for such self-obsession. "God isn't pleased at being ignored" (Rom. 8:8 MSG). Paul speaks of sinners when he describes those who

knew God, but they wouldn't worship him as God or even give him thanks. And they began to think up foolish ideas of what God was like. The result was that their minds became dark and confused. . . .

So God let them go ahead and do whatever shameful things their hearts desired. As a result, they did vile and degrading things with each other's bodies. (Rom. 1:21, 24)

You've seen the chaos. The husband ignoring his wife. The dictator murdering the millions. Grown men seducing the young. The young propositioning the old. When you do what you want, and I do what I want, and no one gives a lick as to what God wants, humanity implodes. The infection of the person leads to the corruption of the populace. As the Puritan clergyman Joseph Alleine wrote: "O miserable man, what a deformed monster has sin made you! God made you 'little lower than the angels'; sin has made you little better than the devils."[1] Extract God; expect earthly chaos and, many times worse, expect eternal misery.

God has made it clear. The plague of sin will not cross his shores. Infected souls never walk his streets. "Unjust people who don't care about God will not be joining in his kingdom. Those who use and abuse each other, use and abuse sex, use and abuse the earth and everything in it, don't qualify as citizens in God's kingdom" (1 Cor. 6:9–10 MSG). God refuses to compromise the spiritual purity of heaven.

Herein lies the awful fruit of sin. Lead a godless life, and expect a godless eternity. Spend a life telling God to leave you alone, and he will. He'll grant you an existence "without God and without hope" (Eph. 2:12). Jesus will "punish those who reject God and who do not obey the Good News about our Lord Jesus. They will suffer the punishment of eternal destruction, separated from the presence of the Lord and from his glorious might" (2 Thess. 1:8–9 TEV).

Christ keeps no secrets about hell. His description purposely chills the soul:

- A place of darkness (Matt. 8:12)

- A fiery furnace (Matt. 13:42)

- A place where "the worm does not die; the fire is never put out" (Mark 9:48 NCV)

Citizens of hell long to die, but cannot. Beg for water, but receive none. They pass into a dawnless night.

So what can we do? If all have been infected and the world is corrupted, to whom do we turn? Or, to re-ask the great question of Scripture: "What must I do to be saved?" (Acts 16:30). The answer offered then is the answer offered still: "Put your entire trust in the Master Jesus" (Acts 16:31 MSG).

Why Jesus? Why not Muhammad or Moses? Joseph Smith or Buddha? What uniquely qualifies Jesus to safeguard the sin-sick? In a sentence: *Christ, the sinless, became sin so that we, the sinners, could be counted sinless.* "God made him who had no sin to be sin for us, so that in him we might become the righteousness of God" (2 Cor. 5:21 NIV). Christ not only became the sin offering by receiving God's wrath for the sins of humanity, he overcame the punishment for sin (death) through his glorious resurrection from the dead.

Life's greatest calamity, from God's perspective, is that people die in sin. In one sentence Christ twice warned, "I told you that you would die in your sins; if you do not believe that I am the one I claim to be, you will indeed die in your sins" (John 8:24 NIV). Forget earthquakes or economic depressions. The ultimate disaster is carrying your sins to your casket. Heaven cannot fathom a worse tragedy. And heaven could not offer a greater gift than this one: "Christ . . . never sinned, but he died for sinners that he might bring us safely home to God" (1 Pet. 3:18).

What if a miracle worker had done something comparable with the Black Plague? Imagine a man born with bubonic resistance. The bacterium can't penetrate his system unless he allows it to do so. And, incredibly, he does. He pursues the infected and makes this offer: "Touch my hand. Give me your disease, and receive my health."

The boil-and-fever-ridden have nothing to lose. They look at his extended hand and reach to touch it. True to the man's word, bacteria pass from their system into his. But their relief spells his anguish. His skin erupts and his body heaves. And as the healed stand in awe, the disease bearer hobbles away.

Our history books tell no such story. But our Bible does.

He took the punishment, and that made us whole.

Through his bruises we get healed. . . .

GOD has piled all our sins, everything we've done wrong

on him, on him. . . .

He took on his own shoulders the sin of the many,

he took up the cause of all the black sheep.

(Isa. 53:5–6, 12 MSG)

Christ responds to universal sin with a universal sacrifice, taking on the sins of the entire world. This is Christ's work *for* you. But God's salvation song has two verses. He not only took your place on the cross; he takes his place in your heart. This is the second stanza: Christ's work *in* you.

"It is no longer I who live," Paul explained, "but Christ lives in me" (Gal. 2:20 NKJV).

Or as he told one church: "Don't you realize that all of you together are the temple of God and that the Spirit of God lives in you?" (1 Cor. 3:16).

In salvation, God enters the hearts of his Adams and Eves. He permanently places himself within us. What powerful implications this brings. "When God lives and breathes in you (and he does, as surely as he did in Jesus), you are delivered from that dead life" (Rom. 8:11 MSG).

Let me show you how this works. It took three hundred years, but the Black Plague finally reached the quaint village of Eyam, England. George Viccars, a tailor, unpacked a parcel shipped from London. The cloth he'd ordered had arrived. But as he opened and shook it, he released plague-infected fleas. Within four days he was dead, and the village was doomed. The town unselfishly quarantined itself, seeking to protect the region.

Other villages deposited food in an open field and left the people of Eyam to die alone. But to everyone's amazement, many survived. A year later, when outsiders again visited the town, they found half the residents had resisted the disease. How so? They had touched it. Breathed it. One surviving mother had buried six children and her husband in one week. The gravedigger had handled hundreds of diseased corpses yet hadn't died. Why not? How did they survive?

Lineage. Through DNA studies of descendants, scientists found proof of a disease-blocking gene. The gene garrisoned the white blood cells, preventing the bacteria from gaining entrance. The plague, in other words, could touch people with this gene but not kill them. Hence a subpopulace swam in a sea of infection but emerged untouched. All because they had the right parents.[2] What's the secret for surviving the Black Plague? Pick the right ancestry.

Of course they couldn't. But by God you can. You can select your spiritual father. You can change your family tree from that of Adam to God. And when you do, he moves in. His resistance becomes your resistance. His Teflon coating becomes yours. Sin may entice you, but will never enslave you. Sin may, and will, touch you, discourage you, and distract you, but it cannot condemn you. Christ is in you, and you are in him, and "there is no condemnation for those who belong to Christ Jesus" (Rom. 8:1).

Can I urge you to trust this truth? Let your constant prayer be this: "Lord, I receive your work. My sins are pardoned." Trust the work of God *for* you. Then trust the presence of Christ *in* you. Take frequent, refreshing drinks from his well of grace. You need regular reminders that you are not fatally afflicted! Don't live as though you are.

A few years ago I noticed a tremor in my left thumb. Upon extension, it shook. I immediately imagined the worst. My father died from Lou Gehrig's disease; my turn was coming. By the time I consulted a doctor, I'd already prepared Denalyn for life as a young widow.

The medical report proved me wrong. No sickness was found. Trace the condition back to caffeine, stress, maybe a family tree, but the doctor informed, "You do not have ALS. You're in good health."

Upon hearing the news, I did what you might expect. I began to weep and asked, "How much time do I have left?"

The doctor cocked his head, puzzled.

"Any chance you could help me break the news to my wife?"

Still he didn't respond. Assuming he was too emotional, I gave him a hug and left.

Stopping at a hospital supply store, I ordered a wheelchair and hospital bed and inquired about home healthcare. I called Denalyn and told her I had some bad news.

Wait a second, you're thinking. *Did you not hear what the doctor told you?*

And I'm wondering, *Did you not hear what heaven told you?*

Christ indwells you! "The blood of Jesus . . . purifies us from all sin" (1 John 1:7 NIV). Then why the guilt on our faces? Why the regret? Why the shadow of shame? Shouldn't we live with a smile and a skip and a sparkle in the eye?

That response to the doctor about my trembling thumb? I made it up. Quite honestly, I gave my physician a handshake, smiled at the receptionist, and called Denalyn with the good news. And now, when I see that thumb shake, I chalk it up to an aging body and place my trust in the doctor's words.

Do the same. For just as my thumb will occasionally tremble, you will occasionally sin. And when you do, remember: sin may touch, but cannot claim you. Christ is in you! Trust his work *for* you. He took your place on the cross. And trust his work *in* you. Your heart is his home, and he is your master.

THREE

When Grace Goes Deep

The prodigal son trudges up the path. His pig stink makes passersby walk wide circles around him, but he doesn't notice. With eyes on the ground, he rehearses his speech: "Father"—his voice barely audible—"I have sinned against heaven and against you. I'm not worthy to be called your son." He rehashes the phrases, wondering if he should say more, less, or make a U-turn to the barnyard. After all, he cashed in the trust fund and trashed the family name. Over the last year, he'd awakened with more parched throats, headaches, women, and tattoos than a rock star. How could his father forgive him? *Maybe I could offer to pay off the credit cards.* He's so focused on penance planning that he fails to hear the sound of his father . . . running!

The dad embraces the mud-layered boy as if he were a returning war hero. He commands the servants to bring a robe, ring, and sandals, as if to say, "No boy of mine is going to look like a pigpen peasant. Fire up the grill. Bring on the drinks. It's time for a party!"

Big brother meanwhile stands on the porch and sulks. "No one ever gave me a party," he mumbles, arms crossed.

The father tries to explain, but the jealous son won't listen. He huffs and shrugs and grumbles something about cheap grace, saddles his high horse, and rides off. But you knew that. You've read the parable of the gracious father and the hostile brother (see Luke 15:11–32).

But have you heard what happened next? Have you read the second chapter? It's a page-turner. The older brother resolves to rain on the forgiveness parade. *If Dad won't exact justice on the boy, I will.*

"Nice robe there, little brother," he tells him one day. "Better keep it clean. One spot and Dad will send you to the cleaners with it."

The younger waves him away, but the next time he sees his father, he quickly checks his robe for stains.

A few days later big brother warns about the ring. "Quite a piece of jewelry Dad gave you. He prefers that you wear it on the thumb."

"The thumb? He didn't tell me that."

"Some things we're just supposed to know."

"But it won't fit my thumb."

"What's your goal—pleasing our father or your own personal comfort?" the spirituality monitor gibes, walking away.

Big brother isn't finished. With the pleasantness of a dyspeptic IRS auditor, he taunts, "If Dad sees you with loose laces, he'll take the sandals back."

"He will not. They were a gift. He wouldn't . . . would he?" The ex-prodigal then leans over to snug the strings. As he does, he spots a smudge on his robe. Trying to rub it off, he realizes the ring is on a finger, not his thumb. That's when he hears his father's voice. "Hello, Son."

There the boy sits, wearing a spotted robe, loose laces, and a misplaced ring. Overcome with fear, he reacts with a "Sorry, Dad" and turns and runs.

Too many tasks. Keeping the robe spotless, the ring positioned, the sandals snug—who could meet such standards? Gift preservation begins to wear on the young man. He avoids the father he feels he can't please. He quits wearing the gifts he can't maintain. And he even begins longing for the simpler days of the pigpen. "No one hounded me there."

That's the rest of the story. Wondering where I found it? On page 1,892 of my Bible, in the book of Galatians. Thanks to some legalistic big brothers, Paul's readers had gone from grace receiving to law keeping. Their Christian life had taken on the joy level of an upper G.I. endoscopy. Paul was puzzled.

I am shocked that you are turning away so soon from God, who in his love and mercy called you to share the eternal life he gives through Christ. You are already following a different way that pretends to be the Good News but is not the Good News at all. You are being fooled by those who twist and change the truth concerning Christ. . . .

And yet we Jewish Christians know that we become right with God, not by doing what the law commands, but by faith in Jesus Christ. So we have believed in Christ Jesus, that we might be accepted by God because of our faith in Christ—and not because we have obeyed the law. For no one will ever be saved by obeying the law. (Gal. 1:6–7; 2:16)

Joy snatchers infiltrated the Roman church as well. Paul had to remind them, "But people are declared righteous because of their faith, not because of their work" (Rom. 4:5).

Philippian Christians heard the same foolishness. Big brothers weren't telling them to wear a ring on their thumb, but they were insisting "you must be circumcised to be saved" (Phil. 3:2).

Even the Jerusalem church, the flagship congregation, heard the solemn monotones of the Quality Control Board. Non-Jewish believers were being told, "You cannot be saved if you are not circumcised as Moses taught us" (Acts 15:1 NCV).

The churches suffered from the same malady: grace blockage. The Father might let you in the gate, but you have to earn your place at the table. God makes the down payment on your redemption, but you pay the monthly installments. Heaven gives the boat, but you have to row it if you ever want to see the other shore.

Grace blockage. Taste, but don't drink. Wet your lips, but never slake your thirst. Can you imagine such instruction over a fountain? "No swallowing, please. Fill your mouth but not your belly."

Absurd. What good is water if you can't drink it? And what good is grace if you don't let it go deep?

Do you? What image best describes your heart? A water-drenched kid dancing in front of an open fire hydrant? Or a bristled desert tumbleweed? Here is how you know. One question. Does God's grace *define* you? Deeply flowing grace clarifies, once and for all, who we are.

But God is so rich in mercy, and he loved us so very much, that even while we were dead because of our sins, he gave us life when he raised Christ from the dead. (It is only by God's special favor that you have been saved!) For he raised us from the dead along with Christ, and we are seated with him in the heavenly realms—all because we are one with Christ Jesus. And so God can always point to us as examples of the incredible wealth of his favor and kindness toward us, as shown in all he has done for us through Christ Jesus.

God saved you by his special favor when you believed. And you can't take credit for this; it is a gift from God. Salvation is not a reward for the good things we have done, so none of us can boast about it. (Eph. 2:4–9)

Look how grace defines us. We are

- spiritually alive: "he gave us life" (v. 5);

- heavenly positioned: "seated with him in the heavenly realms" (v. 6);

- connected to God: "one with Christ Jesus" (v. 6);

- billboards of mercy: "examples of the incredible wealth of his favor and kindness toward us" (v. 7);

- honored children: "God saved you by his special favor" (v. 8).

Grace defines you. As grace sinks in, earthly labels fade. Society labels you like a can on an assembly line. Stupid. Unproductive. Slow learner. Fast talker. Quitter. Cheapskate. But as grace infiltrates, criticism disintegrates. You know you aren't who they say you are. You are who God says you are. Spiritually alive. Heavenly positioned. Connected to the Father. A billboard of mercy. An honored child.

Of course, not all labels are negative. Some people regard you as handsome, clever, successful, or efficient. But even a White House office doesn't compare with being "seated with him in the heavenly realms." Grace creates the Christian's résumé.

It certainly did so for Mephibosheth. Talk about a redefined life. After assuming the throne of Saul, "David began wondering if anyone in Saul's family was still alive, for he had promised Jonathan that he would show kindness to them" (2 Sam. 9:1).

The Philistines, you'll remember, defeated Saul in battle. After the smoke of conflict passed, David sought to display mercy to Saul's descendants. A servant named Ziba remembered: "Yes, one of Jonathan's sons is still alive, but he is crippled" (v. 3). No name offered. Just the pain. Labeled by misfortune. An earlier chapter reveals the mishap. When word of Saul's and Jonathan's deaths reached the capital, a nurse in Jonathan's house swept up his five-year-old boy and fled. But in her haste, she stumbled and dropped him, crippling the boy in both feet.

Where does such a child turn? Can't walk. Can't work. Father and grandfather dead. Where can the crippled grandson of a failed leader go?

How about Lo-debar? Sounds like a place charm forgot. Like No Trees, Texas, or Weed, Oregon, or French Lick, Indiana. Lo-debar, Israel. Appropriate place for Mephibosheth. Stuck with a name longer than his arm. Dropped like a cantaloupe from a torn paper sack. How low can you go? Low enough to end up living in the low-rent district of Lo-debar.

Acquainted with its streets? If you've been dropped, you are. Dropped from the list. Dropped by a guy. Dropped by the team. Dropped off at the orphanage. And now you walk with a limp. People don't remember your name, but they remember your pain. "He's the alcoholic." "Oh, I remember her. The widow." "You mean the divorced woman from Nowheresville?" "No. Lo-debarville." You live labeled.

But then something Cinderella-like happens. The king's men knock on your Lo-debar door. They load you in a wagon and carry you into the presence of the king. You assume the worst and begin praying for a nonsnoring prison cellmate. But the servants don't deposit you on the jailhouse steps; they set you at the king's table. Right above your plate sits a place card bearing your name. "And from that time on, Mephibosheth ate regularly with David, as though he were one of his own sons" (2 Sam. 9:11).

Charles Swindoll has penned a galaxy of fine paragraphs. But my favorite is this imagined scene from David's palace.

> Gold and bronze fixtures gleam from the walls. Lofty, wooden ceilings crown each spacious room. . . . David and his children gather for an evening meal. Absalom, tanned and handsome, is there, as is David's beautiful daughter Tamar. The call to dinner is given, and the king scans the room to see if all are present. One figure, though, is absent.
>
> *Clump, scraaape, clump, scraaape.* The sound coming down the hall echoes into the chamber. *Clump, scraaape, clump, scraaape.* Finally, the person appears at the door and slowly shuffles to his seat. It is the lame Mephibosheth seated in grace at David's table. And the tablecloth covers his feet. Now the feast can begin.[1]

From Lo-debar to the palace, from obscurity to royalty, from no future to the king's table. Quite a move for Mephibosheth. Quite a reminder for us. He models our journey. God lifted us from the dead-end street of Lo-debarville and sat us at his table. "We are seated with him in the heavenly realms" (Eph. 2:6).

Marinate your soul in that verse. Next time the arid desert winds blow, defining you by yesterday's struggles, reach for God's goblet of grace and drink. Grace defines who you are. The parent you can't please is as mistaken as the doting uncle you can't disappoint. People hold no clout. Only God does. According to him, you are his. Period. "For we are God's masterpiece. He has created us anew in Christ Jesus, so that we can do the good things he planned for us long ago" (Eph. 2:10).

Suppose Mephibosheth had seen this verse. Imagine someone back in the Lo-debar days telling him, "Don't be discouraged, friend. I know you can't dance or run. Others kick the soccer ball, and you're stuck here staring out the window. But listen, God wrote your story. He cast you in his drama. Three thousand years from now your story will stir an image of grace for some readers in the twenty-first century."

Would he have believed it? I don't know. But I pray that you will. You hang as God's work of art, a testimony in his gallery of grace.

Over a hundred years ago, a group of fishermen were relaxing in the dining room of a Scottish seaside inn, trading fish stories. One of the men gestured widely, depicting the size of a fish that got away. His arm struck the serving maid's tea tray, sending the teapot flying into the whitewashed wall, where its contents left an irregular brown splotch.

The innkeeper surveyed the damage and sighed, "The whole wall will have to be repainted."

"Perhaps not," offered a stranger. "Let me work with it."

Having nothing to lose, the proprietor consented. The man pulled pencils, brushes, some jars of linseed oil, and pigment out of an art box. He sketched lines around the stains and dabbed shades and colors throughout the splashes of tea. In time, an image began to emerge: a stag with a great rack of antlers. The man inscribed his signature at the bottom, paid for his meal, and left. His name: Sir Edwin Landseer, famous painter of wildlife.

In his hands, a mistake became a masterpiece.[2]

God's hands do the same, over and over. He draws together the disjointed blotches in our life and renders them an expression of his love. We become pictures: "examples of the incredible wealth of his favor and kindness toward us" (Eph. 2:7).

Who determines your identity? What defines you? The day you were dropped? Or the day you were carried to the King's table?

Receive God's work. Drink deeply from his well of grace. As grace sinks deep into your soul, Lo-debar will become a dot in the rearview mirror. Dark days will define you no more. You're in the palace now.

And now you know what to say to the big brothers of this world. No need for frantic robe cleaning or rules for ring wearing. Your deeds don't save you. And your deeds don't keep you saved. Grace does. The next time big brother starts dispensing more snarls than twin Dobermans, loosen your sandals, set your ring on your finger, and quote the apostle of grace who said, "By the grace of God I am what I am" (1 Cor. 15:10 NKJV).

When Death Becomes Birth

What would you do to sidestep death? Upon hearing the footsteps of the Grim Reaper at your door, what price would you pay for an extension? Would you give your right hand?

Aron Ralston did. The twenty-seven-year-old adventurer makes holiday treks out of climbing Rocky Mountain peaks. He's summited forty-five of them, alone, all in winter, most after midnight. Life on the edge isn't new to him. But life beneath an eight-hundred-pound boulder? He was climbing off one when it shifted, trapping his right hand against the wall of a narrow crevice in a remote Utah canyon.

He shoved the rock with his shoulder and tried to chisel it with his knife; he even attempted to hoist the thing with his climbing rope and pulley. The boulder didn't budge. After five days, with food and water gone and having drifted back and forth between depression and visions of friends and margaritas, he made a decision, the thought of which makes mere mortals gulp. He resolved to sever his right hand.

"It occurred to me that if I could break my bones up at the wrist, where they were trapped, I could be freed," he later said. "I was able to first snap the radius and then within another few minutes snap the ulna." Next, with a cheap multiuse tool, the kind that comes with a fifteen-dollar flashlight, he began sawing into his own skin. The blade was so dull it "wouldn't even cut my arm hairs," but he persisted in the amputation. He later told reporters, "It took about an hour."[1]

Don't even imagine the pops and snaps of those sixty minutes. I grow faint when the nurse takes ten seconds to draw my blood.

Ralston finally broke free of the boulder. (Sorry. Poor verb choice.) He now faced the challenge of finding human beings. He crawled through a 150-foot ravine, rappelled (one-handed, remember) down a 60-foot wall, and then hiked six miles. Only then did he run into some Dutch tourists who, no doubt, got more for their money than their travel agent ever promised. Downplaying his courage, Ralston explained the escape as a "matter of pragmatics."[2]

Pragmatic indeed. On one hand, death. Without the other hand, life. When faced with the choice, he chose life. Would we do the same?

We do everything short of it. Death is Public Enemy Number One. Buckle up. Sleep more. Run regularly. Eat less fat. More protein. Less caffeine. More vegetables. Ducking the shadow of death dominates our days.

But no one ducks it forever. Regarding death, Scripture offers some grim facts.

> Some people die in the prime of life,
>   with everything going for them—
>   fat and sassy.

Others die bitter and bereft,

never getting a taste of happiness.

They're laid out side by side in the cemetery,

where the worms can't tell one from the other.

(Job 21:23–26 MSG)

Ecclesiastes 8:8 is equally uplifting. "None of us can hold back our spirit from departing. None of us has the power to prevent the day of our death. There is no escaping that obligation, that dark battle."

This troubles us. We'd appreciate some say-so regarding our death. Couldn't God let us sign up for a departure date? Most would request the one-hundred-year package of good health followed by a long nap from which we wake up in heaven.

God, however, didn't delegate death's datebook. For reasons undisclosed, he runs it without our advice. But while the date of your death isn't revealed, its inevitability is. "It is destined that each person dies only once and after that comes judgment" (Heb. 9:27).

The Utah mountain climber isn't the only one caught between a rock and a hard place. "What man can live and not see death?" (Ps. 89:48 NKJV). You won't find one in your mirror. You, as all God's children, live one final breath from your own funeral.

Which, from God's perspective, is nothing to grieve. He responds to these grave facts with this great news: "The day you die is better than the day you are born" (Eccles. 7:1). Now there is a twist. Heaven enjoys a maternity-ward reaction to funerals. Angels watch body burials the same way grandparents monitor delivery-room doors. "He'll be coming through any minute!" They can't wait to see the new arrival. While we're driving hearses and wearing black, they're hanging pink and blue streamers and passing out cigars. We don't grieve when babies enter the world. The hosts of heaven don't weep when we leave it.

Oh, but many of us weep at the thought of death. Do you? Do you dread your death? And is your dread of death robbing your joy of life? It can. It did for a young woman named Florence. At the age of thirty-seven she told her friends that her life hung by a thread that might snap at any moment. So she went to bed. And stayed there. For fifty-three years! Her death declaration proved true. She did die . . . at the age of ninety.

Doctors could find nothing wrong. Examiners left her bedside shaking their heads. Most diagnosed her as a hopeless hypochondriac—dreading death, ever obsessed by its imminence. Except for three years, Florence cowered before the giant of death. But during those three years on the Crimean battlefront, she made a name for herself, not as one who suffered, but as a friend of those who did. History's most famous nurse, Florence Nightingale, lived as a slave of death.[3]

What about you? Is your fear of dying robbing your joy of living? Then drink up! After all, Jesus came to "deliver those who have lived all their lives as slaves to the fear of dying" (Heb. 2:15).

Death sits well within his jurisdiction. Morticians answer to him. "Christ died and rose again for this very purpose, so that he might be Lord of those who are alive and of those who have died" (Rom. 14:9). Your death may surprise you and sadden others, but heaven knows no untimely death: "You saw me before I was born. Every day of my life was recorded in your book. Every moment was laid out before a single day had passed" (Ps. 139:16).

God dispenses days the way a store clerk dispenses change. For all who doubt his power, Jesus has three words: "Lazarus, come out!" (John 11:43).

If Scripture boasted a list of the famous dead, Lazarus would be near the top. He lived in Bethany, a sleepy hamlet that sat a short walk from Jerusalem. Jesus spent a lot of time there. Maybe he liked the kitchen of Martha or the devotion of Mary. One thing is for sure: he considered Lazarus a friend. News of Lazarus's death prompts Jesus to say, "Our friend Lazarus has fallen asleep, but now I will go and wake him up" (John 11:11).

And now, four days after the funeral, Jesus has come calling. Literally calling, "Lazarus, come out!" Can we try to picture Lazarus as he hears those words? Heaven-sent Lazarus. Heaven-happy Lazarus. Four days into his measureless days. By now he's forming fast friendships with other saints. King David shows him the harps. Moses invites him over for tea and manna. Elijah and Elisha take him for a spin in the fiery chariot. Daniel has promised him a lion of a Bible story. He's on his way to hear it when a voice booms through the celestial city.

"Lazarus, come out!"

Everybody knows that voice. No one wonders, *Who was that?* Angels stop. Hosts of holy-city dwellers turn toward the boy from Bethany, and someone says, "Looks like you're going back for another tour of duty."

Lazarus doesn't question the call. Perfect understanding comes with a heavenly passport. He doesn't object. But had he done so, who could have faulted him? His heavenly body knows no fever. His future no fear. He indwells a city that is void of padlocks, prisons, and Prozac. With sin and death nonexistent, preachers, doctors, and lawyers are free to worship. Would anyone blame Lazarus for saying, "Do I have to go back?"

But he doesn't second-guess the command. Nor does anyone else. Return trips have been frequent of late. The daughter of the synagogue ruler. The boy from Nain. Now Lazarus from Bethany. Lazarus turns toward the rarely used exit door. The very one, I suppose, Jesus used some thirty earth years earlier. With a wave and within a wink, he's reunited with his body and waking up on a cold slab in a wall-hewn grave. The rock to the entrance has been moved, and Lazarus attempts to do the same. Mummy-wrapped, he stiffly sits up and walks out of the tomb with the grace of Frankenstein's monster.

People stare and wonder.

We read and may ask, "Why did Jesus let him die only to call him back?"

To show who runs the show. To trump the cemetery card. To display the unsquashable strength of the One who danced the Watusi on the neck of the devil, who stood face to clammy face with death and declared, "You call that a dead end? I call it an escalator."

"Lazarus, come out!"

Those words, incidentally, were only a warmup for the big day. He's preparing a worldwide grave evacuation. "Joe, come out!" "Maria, come out!" "Giuseppe, come out!" "Jacob, come out!" Grave after grave will empty. What happened to Lazarus will happen to us. Only our spirit-body reunion will occur in heaven, not Bethany Memorial Cemetery.

When this happens—when our perishable earthly bodies have been transformed into heavenly bodies that will never die—then at last the Scriptures will come true:

"Death is swallowed up in victory.

O death, where is your victory?

O death, where is your sting?"

(1 Cor. 15:54–55)

Till then, where does that leave us? It leaves us checking our list of friends. Because Lazarus called Jesus his friend, Jesus called Lazarus from the grave. Regarding death, you need a friend in the highest place. Without one, you're in big trouble. "When the wicked die, their hopes all perish, for they rely on their own feeble strength" (Prov. 11:7). Make sure Jesus refers to you with the same term of endearment he used with Lazarus. Prepare for death by making friends with Christ. "When they arrive at the gates of death, GOD welcomes those who love him" (Ps. 116:15 MSG).

Dread of death ends when you know heaven is your true home. In all my air travels I've never seen one passenger weep when the plane landed. Never. No one clings to the armrests and begs, "Don't make me leave. Don't make me leave. Let me stay and eat more peanuts." We're willing to exit because the plane has no permanent mailing address. Nor does this world. "But we are citizens of heaven, where the Lord Jesus Christ lives. And we are eagerly waiting for him to return as our Savior" (Phil. 3:20).

John Knox could relate. Born in 1505 in Scotland, his preaching regenerated a society. He inspired the masses and defied the excesses of the throne. Some loved him, others despised him, but Scotland has never forgotten him. To this day you can visit his home in Edinburgh and stand in the room where some believe he took his final breath.

Here is what happened. His coworker Richard Bannatyne stood near his bedside. Knox's breath became labored and slow. Bannatyne leaned over his friend's form. "The time to end your battle has come. Have you hope?" he whispered to his friend.

The answer from the old reformer came in the form of a finger. He lifted his finger and pointed it upward and died, inspiring a poet to write:

... the death angel left him, what time earth's bonds were riven,

the cold, stark, stiffening finger still pointing up to heaven.[4]

May your death find you pointing in the same direction. Why don't you do this: give God your death. Imagine your last breath, envision your final minutes, and offer them to him. Deliberately. Regularly. "Lord, I receive your work on the cross and in your resurrection. I entrust you with my departure from earth." With Christ as your friend and heaven as your home, the day of death becomes sweeter than the day of birth.

FIVE

With Heart Headed Home

Search the faces of the Cap Haitian orphanage for Carinette. Study the fifty-seven dark-skinned, bright-eyed, curly-haired, Creole-speaking, fun-loving children for a unique seven-year-old girl. She appears no different from the others. Eats the same rice and beans. Plays on the same grassless playground. Sleeps beneath a tin roof as do the other girls, hearing the nearly nightly pounding of the Haitian rain. But though she appears the same, don't be fooled. She lives in a different world—a world called home-to-be.

See the slender girl wearing the pink shirt? The girl with the long nose and bushy hair and a handful of photos. Ask to see them; Carinette will let you. Fail to ask; she'll show you anyway. The photos bear the images of her future family. She's been adopted.

Her adoptive parents are friends of mine. They brought her pictures, a teddy bear, granola bars, and cookies. Carinette shared the goodies and asked the director to guard her bear, but she keeps the pictures. They remind her of her home-to-be. Within a month, two at the most, she'll be there. She knows the day is coming. Every opening of the gate jumps her heart. Any day now her father will appear. He promised he'd be back. He came once to claim her. He'll come again to carry her home.

Till then she lives with a heart headed home.

Shouldn't we all? Carinette's situation mirrors ours. Our Father paid us a visit too. Have we not been claimed? Adopted? "So you should not be like cowering, fearful slaves. You should behave instead like God's very own children, adopted into his family— calling him 'Father, dear Father'" (Rom. 8:15).

God searched you out. Before you knew you needed adopting, he'd already filed the papers and selected the wallpaper for your room. "For God knew his people in advance, and he chose them to become like his Son, so that his Son would be the firstborn, with many brothers and sisters" (Rom. 8:29).

Abandon you to a fatherless world? No way. Those privy to God's family Bible can read your name. He wrote it there. What's more, he covered the adoption fees. Neither you nor Carinette can pay your way out of the orphanage, so "God sent [Christ] to buy freedom for us who were slaves to the law, so that he could adopt us as his very own children" (Gal. 4:5).

We don't finance our adoption, but we do accept it. Carinette could tell the prospective parents to get lost. But she hasn't. In the same way, you could tell God to get lost. But you wouldn't dare, would you? The moment we accept his offer we go from orphans to heirs.

"Heirs of God and joint heirs with Christ" (Rom. 8:17 NKJV). Heirs! Heaven knows no stepchildren or grandchildren. You and Christ share the same will. What he inherits, you inherit. You are headed home.

Oh, but we forget. Don't we grow accustomed to hard bunks

and tin plates? Seldom do we peer over the fence into the world to come. And how long has it been since you showed someone your pictures? Is Peter speaking to you when he urges, "Friends, this world is not your home, so don't make yourselves cozy in it" (1 Pet. 2:11 MSG)?

Adopted, but not transported. We have a new family, but not our heavenly house. We know our Father's name, but we haven't seen his face. He has claimed us, but has yet to come for us.

So here we are. Caught between what is and what will be. No longer orphans, but not yet home. What do we do in the meantime? Indeed, it can be just that—a *mean* time. Time made mean with chemotherapy, drivers driving with more beer than brains in their bodies, and backstabbers who make life on earth feel like a time-share in Afghanistan. How do we live in the *mean*time? How do we keep our hearts headed home? Paul weighs in with some suggestions.

> And even we Christians, although we have the Holy Spirit within us as a foretaste of future glory, also groan to be released from pain and suffering. We, too, wait anxiously for that day when God will give us our full rights as his children, including the new bodies he has promised us. Now that we are saved, we eagerly look forward to this freedom. For if you already have something, you don't need to hope for it. But if we look forward to something we don't have yet, we must wait patiently and confidently. (Rom. 8:23–25)

Paul calls the Holy Spirit a foretaste. "We have the Holy Spirit . . . as a foretaste of future glory" (v. 23). No person with a healthy appetite needs a definition for that word. Even as I draft this chapter, my mind drifts toward a few foretastes. Within an hour

I'll be in Denalyn's kitchen sniffing the dinner trimmings like a Labrador sniffing for wild game. When she's not looking, I'll snatch a foretaste. Just a bite of turkey, a spoon of chili, a corner of bread . . . predinner snacks stir appetites for the table.

Samplings from heaven's kitchen do likewise. There are moments, perhaps far too few, when time evaporates and joy modulates and heaven hands you an hors d'oeuvre.

- Your newborn has passed from restlessness to rest. Beneath the amber light of a midnight moon, you trace a soft finger across tiny, sleeping eyes and wonder, *God gave you to me?* A prelibation from heaven's winery.

- You're lost in the work you love to do, were made to do. As you step back from the moist canvas or hoed garden or rebuilt V-eight engine, satisfaction flows within like a gulp of cool water, and the angel asks, "Another apéritif?"

- The lyrics to the hymn say what you couldn't but wanted to, and for a moment, a splendid moment, there are no wars, wounds, or tax returns. Just you, God, and a silent assurance that everything is right with the world.

Rather than dismiss or disregard such moments as good luck, relish them. They can attune you to heaven. So can tough ones. "Although we have the Holy Spirit within us as a foretaste of future glory, [we] also groan to be released from pain and suffering. We, too, wait anxiously for that day when God will give us our full rights as his children, including the new bodies he has promised us" (v. 23).

Do you think Carinette groans? Orphans tend to. They live

lonely lives. Upon seeing a child with a mother and father, they groan. They see a house and think of their bunk; they groan. When they wonder what happened to their biological parents, wouldn't they groan? Of course.

But Carinette's groans are numbered. Every cafeteria meal brings her closer to home cooking, and each dormitory night carries her closer to a room of her own. And every time she longs to call someone mama, she remembers that she soon will.

Her struggles stir longings for home. Let your bursitis-plagued body remind you of your eternal one; let acid-inducing days prompt thoughts of unending peace. Are you falsely accused? Acquainted with abuse? Mudslinging is a part of this life, but not the next. Rather than begrudge life's troubles, listen to them.

Certain moments are so hideous, nothing else will do. A few years ago a *Time* magazine essay escorted readers into the ugly world of abused children. We met Antwan, age ten, puppet-stringed to neighborhood bullies and drug peddlers. They demanded his presence. He feared their punishment. When police appeared, the troublemakers stashed their drugs in his socks, thinking the boy wouldn't be searched. Antwan knew the police better than he knew his schoolteachers. What hope does a boy like Antwan have? The writer took us to his sparse apartment. His mother owned one light bulb. When she left the kitchen, she carried the lone bulb to the living room. As she screwed it into the lamp, the dim glow illuminated a poster on a far wall of a young black boy crying. The caption at the bottom read, "He will wipe away all tears from their eyes, and there shall be no more death, nor sorrow, nor crying, nor pain. All of that has gone forever" (Rev. 21:4 TLB).[1]

Write checks of hope on this promise. Do not bemoan passing time; applaud it. The more you drink from God's well, the more you urge the clock to tick. Every bump of the second hand brings you closer to a completed adoption. As Paul writes, "We, too, wait anxiously for that day when God will give us our full rights as his children" (Rom. 8:23).

My daughters have long since stopped doing this, but there was a time when they celebrated my daily arrival. Jenna was five years old, Andrea three. Denalyn would alert them, and they would scamper to the window, pressing noses and hands against the tall pane that paralleled the front door. As I pulled into the drive, I would see them: Andrea and Jenna, a head taller than her sister, squeezed into the frame. Seeing me, they squealed. My, how they jumped and clapped. You'd think someone had switched their M&M's for coffee beans. No returning Caesar ever felt more welcomed. As I opened the door, they tackled my knees and flooded the entryway with tsunami-size joy.

Their father was home.

It's been too long since I searched for God that way. Too seldom do I hear thunder and think, *Is that God?* I've been known to let a day, even two, pass without a glance to the eastern sky. Let's do better. "Let heaven fill your thoughts. Do not think only about things down here on earth" (Col. 3:2). How about regular ladle dips into the well of God's return? Don't you know Carinette's home-to-be dominates her thoughts? The pictures, the teddy bear—can she see them and not think of it?

Blessings and burdens. Both can alarm-clock us out of slumber. Gifts stir homeward longings. So do struggles. Every homeless day carries us closer to the day our Father will come.

Part Two

Rely on His

Energy

SIX

Hope for Tuckered Town

Turn north at Stress Village, drive a few miles east of Worryville, bear right at the fork leading through Worn-Out Valley, and you'll find yourself entering the weary streets of Tuckered Town.

Her residents live up to the name. They lumber like pack mules on a Pike's Peak climb. Eyes down. Faces long. Shoulders slumped. Ask them to explain their sluggish ways, and they point to the cars. "You'd be tired too if you had to push one of these."

To your amazement that's what they do! Shoulders pressing, feet digging, lungs puffing, they muscle automobiles up and down the street. Rather than sit behind the wheel, they lean into the trunk.

The sight puzzles you. The sound stuns you. Do you hear what you think you hear? Running engines. Citizens of Tuckered Town turn the key, start the car, slip it into neutral, and shove!

You have to ask someone why. A young mother rolls her minivan into the grocery store parking lot. "Ever thought of pressing the gas?" you question.

"I do," she replies, brushing sweat away. "I press the gas to start the car; then I take over."

A bizarre answer. But no more bizarre than that of the out-of-breath fellow leaning against his eighteen-wheeler, wheezing like an overweight marathoner. "Did you push this truck?" you ask.

"I did," he gasps, covering his mouth with an oxygen mask.

"Why not use your accelerator?"

He cocks an eyebrow. "Because I'm a Tucker trucker, and we're strong enough to do our own work."

He doesn't look strong to you. But you say nothing. Just walk away wondering, *What kind of people are these? A pedal push away from power, yet they ignore it. Who would live in such a way?*

Paul asked the Galatian church an identical question. "You began your life in Christ by the Spirit. Now are you trying to make it complete by your own power? That is foolish" (Gal. 3:3 NCV). Is God nothing more than a jumper cable? Start-up strength and nothing more?

Corinthian Christians pushed a few cars too. "You are still not spiritual," the apostle accused (1 Cor. 3:3 NCV). What are you saying, Paul? Are they saved? Yes. He addresses them as "brothers and sisters" (1 Cor. 3:1 NCV). He considers them to be God's children. Heaven bound. Saved, but not spiritual. Plugged in, but not flipped on. "Brothers and sisters . . . I had to talk to you as I would to people without the Spirit—babies in Christ. . . . You are still not spiritual, because there is jealousy and quarreling among you, and this shows that you are not spiritual. You are acting like people of the world" (1 Cor. 3:1–3 NCV).

I used to think there were two kinds of people: the saved and unsaved. Paul corrects me by describing a third: the *saved, but unspiritual*. The spiritual person is Spirit dependent, Spirit directed,

Spirit dominated. He seeks to "walk in the Spirit" (Gal. 5:16 NKJV). Conversely, the unspiritual person cranks the car and hunkers behind it. Tragically, these people act "like people of the world" (1 Cor. 3:3 NCV). In language, lifestyle, priorities, and personality, they blend in with nonbelievers. They let God save them, but not change them.

Such carnal Christianity frustrates Paul. "You began your life in Christ by the Spirit. Now are you trying to make it complete by your own power? That is foolish" (Gal. 3:3 NCV).

Foolish and miserable. You don't want to carpool with unspiritual Christians. They have no kind words to share. "There is jealousy and strife" among them (1 Cor. 3:3 NASB). The only joy they know graduated from high school last year. And gratitude? Gratitude for what? The two-ton Hummer that daily has to be pushed uphill? The saved but unspiritual see salvation the way a farmer sees a hundred acres of untilled soil—lots of work. *Church attendance, sin resistance—have I done enough?* No wonder they're tired. No wonder they argue. "You are jealous of one another and quarrel with each other. Doesn't that prove you are controlled by your own desires?" (1 Cor. 3:3).

> Harsh words
> Joyless days
> Contentious relationships
> Thirsty hearts

You'll find more excitement at an Amish prom. Who wants to live in Tuckered Town? Moreover, who wants to move there? Nothing repels non-Christians more than gloomy Christians. No one wants a free truck if you have to push it. Your neighbor doesn't.

You don't. And God doesn't want it for any of us. He never intended for you to perambulate your life.

His word for tuckered-out Christians? "As you received Christ Jesus the Lord, so continue to live in him" (Col. 2:6 NCV).

How does one receive Christ? By coming thirsty and drinking deeply. How, then, does one live in Christ? By coming thirsty and drinking deeply.

When you do, saving power becomes staying power. "God, who began the good work within you, will continue his work until it is finally finished on that day when Christ Jesus comes back again" (Phil. 1:6).

Christ did not give you a car and tell you to push it. He didn't even give you a car and tell you to drive it. You know what he did? He threw open the passenger door, invited you to take a seat, and told you to buckle up for the adventure of your life.

When Christ enters the Tuckered Towns of the world, he stands at the intersection of Dead-Tired Avenue and Done-In Street and compels, "'If you are thirsty, come to me! If you believe in me, come and drink! For the Scriptures declare that rivers of living water will flow out from within.' (When he said 'living water,' he was speaking of the Spirit, who would be given to everyone believing in him)" (John 7:37–39).

"Come to me!" Not "come to my church" or "come to my system," but "come to me!"

Come to me and drink. No sipping. No tasting. It's time to chug-a-lug. Thirsty throats gulp water. Thirsty souls gulp Christ. The margin notes of the New American Standard Bible state: "Keep coming to Me and . . . keep drinking." Annual fill-ups or monthly ingestions won't do. You aren't sampling wine at a California vineyard. You're hiking through Death Valley, and that mirage you see is not a mirage but really is the river you need. Dive in and drink.

And as you do, look what happens: "rivers of living water will flow out from within" (John 7:38). The word for *rivers* can be translated *floods* (see Matt. 7:25, 27; Rev. 12:15–16). We've seen torrents torrential enough to carry homes. Newscasts run and rerun images of a house floating downstream. What is this force that can float a house?

One smaller than the power who floods you. "He was speaking of the Spirit, who would be given to everyone believing in him" (John 7:39). God's Spirit. God's powerful, unseen, undeniable presence pulsating through heart canals. A "spring of water gushing up inside that person, giving eternal life" (John 4:14 NCV).

God's Spirit rages within you. Whether you feel him or not is unimportant. Whether you understand him is insignificant. Jesus said, "Living water will flow out from within" (7:38). Not "may flow," "could flow," or "has been known to flow." But "will flow."

If such is the case, Max, then explain my weariness and irritability. If God's Spirit lives within me, why do I have the compassion of Hermann Goering? I can't tolerate my mother or control my temper or forgive myself. I'm so tired.

God through Paul answers that question with five rich words: "Be filled with the Spirit" (Eph. 5:18 NCV). The verb tense caused original readers to see capital letters: BE FILLED. With the same imperative gusto that he instructs, "Forgive," "Pray," and "Speak truth," God commands, "BE FILLED."

Not only does Paul give a command; he gives a continuous, collective command. Continuous in the sense that the filling is a daily privilege. Collective because the invitation is offered to all people. "You *all* be filled with the Spirit." Young, old, servants, businessmen, seasoned saints, and new converts. The Spirit will fill all. No SAT (Spiritual Aptitude Test) required. You don't need to persuade him to enter; he already has. Better set another plate for dinner. You've got company. "Your body is a temple for the Holy Spirit who is in you" (1 Cor. 6:19 NCV). As a Christian, you have all the power you need for all the problems you face.

The real question is not, how do I get more of the Spirit? but rather, how can you, Spirit, have more of me? We'd expect a Mother Teresa–size answer to that question. Build an orphanage. Memorize Leviticus. Bathe lepers. Stay awake through a dozen Lucado books. *Do this and be filled,* we think.

"Do this on your own and be tired," God corrects. Do you desire God's Spirit? Here is what you do. Ask. "Everyone who asks will receive. . . . You know how to give good things to your children. How much more your heavenly Father will give the Holy Spirit to those who ask him!" (Luke 11:10, 13 NCV).

The Spirit fills as prayers flow. Desire to be filled with strength? Of course you do. Then pray, "Lord, I receive your energy. Empowered by your Holy Spirit, I can do all things through Christ, who gives me strength." Welcome the Spirit into every room of your heart.

I did something similar with the air of my air conditioner. As I study in my dining room, cool air surrounds me. Outside the sidewalk sizzles in brick-oven heat. But inside I'm as cool as the other side of the pillow. Why? Two reasons. A compressor sits next to the house. I did not build nor install it. It came with the mortgage. Credit the cool house on a good compressor.

But equally credit the open vents. I did not install the "air makers," but I did open the "air blockers." Cool air fills the house because vents are open. I went from room to room, lowering the levers and releasing the air. The Holy Spirit will fill your life as you do the same: as you, room by room, invite him to flow in.

Try this: before you climb out of bed, mentally escort the Spirit into every room of your house. Before your feet touch the floor, open each vent. Got anger in a bedroom? Unpayable bills on a desk? Conflicts in an office? Need some air in the cellar or a change of atmosphere in the hallways? Invite him to fill each corridor of your life. Then, having welcomed him into your whole heart, go to your garage, climb into the passenger seat, buckle up, and thank your Driver that you don't live in Tuckered Town anymore.

SEVEN

Waiting for Power

Buried like a grass burr in Matthew's rose bed is this disclosure: "Then the eleven disciples left for Galilee, going to the mountain where Jesus had told them to go. When they saw him, they worshiped him—but *some of them still doubted!*" (Matt. 28:16–17, emphasis mine). Three years of miracles weren't enough. Nor were forty days at the Resurrection Retreat Center. They've seen him vacate tombs and dictate weather patterns, but still they doubt.

You have to be kidding. Who knows him better than they? Ask them a Christ question. Go ahead. Anything. Did he hum as he walked? Pray before he ate? Did he talk to storms in his sleep? And, if he did, did storms listen? They know. They know the person of Christ.

And, my, how they could speak on the passion of Christ. John winced as the hammer clanged. Mary wept as her son groaned. Close enough to be splattered by his blood, they knew his passion. When it came time to prepare the body for burial, they did.

And when it came time to see the empty tomb, they did that,

too. Peter ran a finger down the stone slab. Thomas studied Christ's pierced hands like a palm reader. And for forty days Jesus taught them. Forty days! Can you imagine a six-week seminar with the mind behind the microbes? "Tell us again, Jesus. Tell us how you got the hell out of hell."

Hand trained by Christ. Witnesses to the hinge moments of history. These folks are ready, aren't they? Apparently not. "Some of them still doubted."

Questions keep buzzing like a summer fly. Even after a thousand campfire conversations and a scrapbook full of jaw-dropping moments, some disciples resist. *I'm still not sure.*

What will Jesus do with them? We'd like to know, wouldn't we? We'd really like to know. *Still* stalks our sentences too.

"I still worry."

"I still gossip."

"Permafrost still chills my marriage."

"I'm still torn between the AA meeting and the corner bar."

"I still clench my teeth every time I get a call from that speck-of-dandruff ex-boyfriend of mine."

We find odd comfort in the lingering doubts of the disciples. For we still have our own. And so we wonder, *Does Christ have a word for those who linger near the dis-*still-*ery of doubt?*

His "yes" resounds. And his instruction will surprise you. What he told them, he tells us. "Don't leave Jerusalem yet. Wait here for the Father to give you the Holy Spirit, just as I told you he has promised to do" (Acts 1:4 CEV).

Jesus's word to the doubting disciples? "Wait." Before you go out, stand still. Prior to stepping forth, sit down. "Stay here in the city until the Holy Spirit comes and fills you with power from heaven" (Luke 24:49).

So they do. "They went to the upstairs room of the house where they were staying. . . . They all met together continually for prayer, along with Mary the mother of Jesus, several other women, and the brothers of Jesus" (Acts 1:13–14).

They have reasons to leave. Someone has a business to run or field to farm. Besides, the same soldiers who killed Christ still walk Jerusalem's streets. The disciples have ample reason to leave . . . but they don't. They stay. And they stay together.

"They all met together continually." As many as 120 souls huddle in the same house. How many potential conflicts exist in this group? Talk about a powder keg. Nathanael might glare at Peter for denying Christ at the fire. Then again, at least Peter stood near the fire. He could resent the others for running. So could the women. Faithful females who stood near the cross share the room with cowardly men who fled the cross. The room is ripe for conflict. Mary could demand special treatment. Jesus's blood brothers are in the room. They once tried to lock up Christ. Who's to say they won't lock up his followers? And the women. Isn't this a men's meeting? Who let the ladies in? Bitterness, arrogance, distrust, chauvinism—the room is a kindling box for all four. But no one strikes a match. They stay together, and most of all, they pray together.

"They all met together continually for prayer." Mark uses the same Greek word here translated "continually" to describe a boat floating in the water, waiting on Jesus. The Master, speaking on the beach of Galilee, told the disciples to have a boat ready and waiting (Mark 3:9). The boat was "continually" in the presence of Christ. So are the Upper Room disciples. One day passes. Then two. Then a week. For all they know a hundred more will come and go. But they aren't leaving. They persist in the presence of Christ.

Then, ten days later, hang on to your turban:

On the day of Pentecost, seven weeks after Jesus' resurrection, the
believers were meeting together in one place. Suddenly, there was
a sound from heaven like the roaring of a mighty windstorm in
the skies above them, and it filled the house where they were
meeting. Then, what looked like flames or tongues of fire
appeared and settled on each of them. And everyone present was
filled with the Holy Spirit. (Acts 2:1–4)

Doubters became prophets. Peter preached, and people came,
and God opened the floodgates on the greatest movement in history. It began because the followers were willing to do one thing:
wait in the right place for power.

We're so reluctant to do what they did. Who has time to wait?
We groan at such a thought. But waiting doesn't mean inactiv-
ity—rather inHIMactivity. Waiting means watching for him. If
you are waiting on a bus, you are watching for the bus. If you are
waiting on God, you are watching for God, searching for God,
hoping in God. Great promises come to those who do. "But those
who wait on the LORD will find new strength. They will fly high
on wings like eagles. They will run and not grow weary. They will
walk and not faint" (Isa. 40:31).

To those who still struggle, God says, "Wait on me." And wait in
the right place. Jesus doesn't tell us to stay in Jerusalem, but he does
tell us to stay honest, stay faithful, stay true. "If you rebel against the
LORD's commands and refuse to listen to him, then his hand will be
as heavy upon you as it was upon your ancestors" (1 Sam. 12:15).
Are you illegally padding your pocket? Are you giving your body to
someone who doesn't share your name and wear your ring? Is your

mouth a Mississippi River of gossip? If you intentionally hang out at the bus stop of disobedience, you need to know something—God's bus doesn't stop there. Go to the place of obedience. "The Holy Spirit . . . is God's gift to those who obey him" (Acts 5:32 TEV).

While you're waiting in the right place, get along with people. Would the Holy Spirit have anointed contentious disciples? According to Peter, disharmony hinders prayers. He tells husbands, "Live with your wives in an understanding way. . . . Do this so that nothing will stop your prayers" (1 Pet. 3:7 NCV). Waiting on God means working through conflicts, forgiving offenses, resolving disputes. "Always keep yourselves united in the Holy Spirit, and bind yourselves together with peace" (Eph. 4:3).

Some years ago our family had a backyard trampoline. One Saturday afternoon I noticed all three of our girls bouncing on it. My daughters, like all siblings, don't always get along. But for some reason, that afternoon they were one another's biggest fans. When one jumped, the other two applauded. If one fell, the other two helped her stand. My chest swelled with pride. After a few moments, you know what I did? I joined them. I couldn't resist. Their alliance pleased me. Our alliance pleases Christ. Jesus promised, "When two or three of you are together because of me, you can be sure that I'll be there" (Matt. 18:20 MSG).

Desire power for your life? It will come as you "do your part to live in peace with everyone, as much as possible" (Rom. 12:18).

It will also come as you pray. For ten days the disciples prayed. Ten days of prayer plus a few minutes of preaching led to three thousand saved souls. Perhaps we invert the numbers. We're prone to pray for a few minutes and preach for ten days. Not the apostles. Like the boat waiting for Christ, they lingered in his presence. They never left the place of prayer.

Biblical writers spoke often of this place. Early Christians were urged to

- "pray without ceasing" (1 Thess. 5:17 NASB);
- "always be prayerful" (Rom. 12:12);
- "pray at all times and on every occasion" (Eph. 6:18).

Remember the adverb *continually* that described the Upper Room prayer of the apostles? It's used to describe our prayers as well: "Continue earnestly in prayer, being vigilant in it with thanksgiving" (Col. 4:2 NKJV).

Sound burdensome? Are you wondering, *My business needs attention, my children need dinner, my bills need paying. How can I stay in a place of prayer?* Unceasing prayer may sound complicated, but it needn't be that way.

Do this. Change your definition of prayer. Think of prayers less as an activity for God and more as an awareness of God. Seek to live in uninterrupted awareness. Acknowledge his presence everywhere you go. As you stand in line to register your car, think, *Thank you, Lord, for being here.* In the grocery as you shop, *Your presence, my King, I welcome.* As you wash the dishes, worship your Maker. Brother Lawrence did. This well-known saint called himself the "lord of pots and pans." In his book *The Practice of the Presence of God*, he wrote:

The time of business does not with me differ from the time of prayer; and in the noise and clatter of my kitchen, while several persons are at the same time calling for different things, I possess God in as great tranquility as if I were upon my knees at the blessed sacrament.[1]

Though a rookie in the League of Unceasing Prayer, I sure enjoy the pursuit. I've discovered the strength of carrying on two conversations: one with a person, another with the Person. One can, at once, listen and petition. As a person unfolds his problem, I'm often silently saying, *God, a little help here, please*. He always provides it. I've also discovered the delight of regular drinks from his water cooler. Throughout the day, my thoughts are marked with phrases: *Guide me, dear Father. Forgive that idea, please. Protect my daughters today*.

A final thought. The Upper Room was occupied by 120 disciples. Since there were about 4,000,000 people in Palestine at the time, this means that fewer than 1 in 30,000 was a Christian.[2] Yet look at the fruit of their work. Better said, look at the fruit of God's Spirit in them. We can only wonder what would happen today if we, who *still* struggle, did what they did: wait on the Lord in the right place.

EIGHT

God's Body Glove

You are so proud of the new gloves you just bought. Your old set was worn and threadbare, defenseless against winter's bite. So you shopped until you found just the right pair. How many did you examine? Dozens. And how many did you try on? Nearly the same number. After all, what good are gloves if you don't like them or they don't fit?

Ah, but then you found these. The clerk did you a favor. She reached under the counter and produced a set still wrapped in plastic. You paid the price and walked out the door, unsealing the bag. And now, walking down the avenue on a chilly morning, you prepare to wear your brand-new gloves.

You step to the side of the foot traffic, tear open the plastic cover, and plunge your hand into the woolen warmth, only to be stopped. You can't get your fingers into the fingers! The five entryways are stitched together. Mistake of the factory? Oversight of the store? Who knows? One thing is certain: your fingers won't fill the glove. A closed fist will, but an extended hand won't.

No problem, you say to yourself. *I'll make do.* You fist your way into the palm and park there, your fingers folded, the glove fingers flopping. Not exactly what you had in mind, but, hey, when it comes to warmth, you can't complain. Folded fingers stay nice and toasty. Frostbite is no concern.

Function, however, is. Ever tried to pick up a newspaper with your fingers folded inside a glove? Not easy. Neither is tying your shoes. Your hands feel like horse hoofs. Wave at someone, and he thinks you are shaking your fist. And forget grabbing a pencil or dialing a cell phone. Floppy wool has no grip.

You want extended fingers, stretched and strong. Why? You have leaves to rake. A steering wheel to grip. A neighbor's hand to shake. Simply put, you have things to do.

So does God. Babies need hugs. Children need good-night tucks. AIDS orphans need homes. Stressed-out executives need hope. God has work to do. And he uses our hands to do it.

What the hand is to the glove, the Spirit is to the Christian. "Behold, I stand at the door and knock; if anyone hears My voice and opens the door, I will *come in* to him" (Rev. 3:20 NASB, emphasis mine). God gets into us. At times, imperceptibly. Other times, disruptively. God gets his fingers into our lives, inch by inch reclaiming the territory that is rightfully his.

Your tongue. He claims it for his message.

Your feet. He requisitions them for his purpose.

Your mind? He made it and intends to use it for his glory.

Your eyes, face, and hands? Through them he will weep, smile, and touch.

As a glove responds to the strength of the hand, so you will respond to the leading of Christ to the point where you say, "I myself no longer live, but Christ lives in me" (Gal. 2:20). Oh, but the process can come so slowly. Why do some walk with such confidence and others stumble with such regularity?

Receiving the unseen is not easy. Most Christians find the cross of Christ easier to accept than the Spirit of Christ. Good Friday makes more sense than Pentecost. Christ, our substitute. Jesus taking our place. The Savior paying for our sins. These are astounding, yet embraceable, concepts. They fall in the arena of transaction and substitution, familiar territory for us. But Holy Spirit discussions lead us into the realm of the supernatural and unseen. We grow quickly quiet and cautious, fearing what we can't see or explain.

It helps to consider the Spirit's work from this angle. What Jesus did in Galilee is what the Holy Spirit does in us. Jesus *dwelt among* the people, teaching, comforting, and convicting. The Holy Spirit *dwells within* us, teaching, comforting, and convicting. The preferred New Testament word for this promise is *oikeo*, which means "live or dwell." *Oikeo* descends from the Greek noun *oikos*, which means "house." The Holy Spirit indwells the believer in the same way a homeowner indwells a house.

> Those who trust God's action in them find that God's Spirit is in them—living and breathing God! . . .
>
> But if God himself has taken up residence in your life, you can hardly be thinking more of yourself than of him. Anyone, of course, who has not welcomed this invisible but clearly present God, the Spirit of Christ, won't know what we're talking about. But for you who welcome him, in whom he dwells—even though you still experience all the limitations of sin—you yourself experience life on God's terms. (Rom. 8:5, 9–10 MSG)

Did you see the phrases of permanence? *God's Spirit is in them. . . . God himself has taken up residence in your life . . . in whom he dwells.* To Timothy, Paul urges, "You have been trusted with a wonderful treasure. Guard it with the help of the Holy Spirit, who lives within you" (2 Tim. 1:14 CEV). Could the apostle's words have been clearer than "Don't you realize that all of you together are the temple of God and that the Spirit of God lives in you?" (1 Cor. 3:16)?

All believers have God in their heart. But not all believers have given their whole heart to God. Remember, the question is not, how can I have more of the Spirit? but rather, how can the Spirit have more of me? A palm and a few fingers will not suffice. C. S. Lewis put it well:

> Christ says, "Give me All. I don't want so much of your time and so much of your money and so much of your work: I want You. I have not come to torment your natural self, but to kill it. No half-measures are any good. I don't want to cut off a branch here and a branch there, I want to have the whole tree down. . . . Hand over the whole natural self, all the desires which you think innocent as well as the desires you think wicked—the whole outfit. I will give you a new self instead. In fact, I will give you Myself: my own will shall become yours."[1]

Take inventory. As you look around your life, do you see any resistant pockets? Any stitched-up fingers? Go down the list.

Your tongue. Do you tend to stretch the truth? Puff up the facts? Your language? Is your language a sewer of profanities and foul talk? And grudges? Do you keep resentments parked in your "garudge"? Are you unproductive and lazy? Do you live off the system, assuming that the church or the country should take care of you?

If you find these questions too personal, blame Paul. He crafted the list.

So put away all falsehood and "tell your neighbor the truth" because we belong to each other. And "don't sin by letting anger gain control over you." Don't let the sun go down while you are still angry, for anger gives a mighty foothold to the Devil.

If you are a thief, stop stealing. Begin using your hands for honest work, and then give generously to others in need. Don't use foul or abusive language. Let everything you say be good and helpful, so that your words will be an encouragement to those who hear them.

And *do not bring sorrow to God's Holy Spirit by the way you live*. Remember, he is the one who has identified you as his own, guaranteeing that you will be saved on the day of redemption.

Get rid of all bitterness, rage, anger, harsh words, and slander, as well as all types of malicious behavior. (Eph. 4:25–31, emphasis mine)

Do your actions interrupt the flow of the Spirit in your life?

Our life was interrupted recently by an uninvited guest. I had turned on the television to watch the baseball play-offs. The reception was erratic. The game appeared and disappeared. I did all the professional stuff, like jiggling the connection and pounding on the set . . . Nothing helped.

The cable company checked the system and determined that the originating signal was strong and that the problem was on my end. A couple of days later a serviceman discovered what was wrong. Denalyn couldn't resist calling me with the news. "Remember the ring-tailed cat we heard scampering in the attic?" she asked.

A week earlier we'd awakened to the pitter-patter of furred feet over our bedroom ceiling. The pest-control guy had found clues of a ring-tailed cat—a little round-faced feline with a bushy tail. He set out a cage, and, sure enough, the sound stopped. To be honest, I thought he'd retrieved the critter. He hadn't. For a day or so, the caged cat sat in the attic.

I knew nothing about caged, ring-tailed cats, but this much I learned. They don't like major-league baseball games. While poor reception was yanking me in and out of Yankee Stadium, he was upstairs chewing on the cable. The wire cage had an opening just large enough for his nose and just close enough to the wire to keep me from seeing Boston beat New York.

Acknowledging pests isn't enough; you have to do something to get them out of the house.

You're likely aware of a few critters of your own: jealousy, bigotry, greed, anxiety. You can hear them scamper. You don't like the sound of them, and you may have even set out a few traps. "I'm working on my temper." "This bad habit needs attention." Good start, but don't stop there. Trapping varmints isn't enough. Call the heavenly pest control. Ask God to help you get rid of them.

Remember Paul's instruction? "Get rid of all bitterness, rage, anger, harsh words, and slander, as well as all types of malicious behavior" (Eph. 4:31). Harbored sin interferes with Spirit circulation. Confessed sin, however, splices the cable and restores the power.

This could take time. Don't give up on it. Don't let stumbles stop you. Come and keep coming. Drink and keep drinking. Ask and keep asking. "Your heavenly Father [will] give the Holy Spirit to those who ask and continue to ask Him!" (Luke 11:13 AMP).

Don't make the mistake of the fly I encountered in the airplane. That's right, on a recent flight a fly buzzed about in the cabin. How odd. A fly flying inside a flying plane. Why would a fly fly during a flight? Was he helping the plane? Doing his part to keep the craft airborne? Why did the fly in the plane fly in the plane?

I asked him. Catching his attention, I inquired, "Mr. Fly, why do you fly? Why don't you sit down and enjoy the journey?"

His reply smacked of smugness. "And let the plane crash? Why, this craft needs me. My wings are essential to our safety." And with a puff of the chest he flew toward the front of the plane. As he returned some moments later, he didn't look so confident. Fear flickered in his tiny eyes. "I don't think I can keep it up!"

"Keep what up?"

"The plane! I don't think I can keep the plane up. I'm flying as furiously as I can. But my wings are weary. I don't know how long I can do this."

I opted for frankness. "Don't you know it's not up to you? You are surrounded by strength, held aloft by power that is not yours. Stop flying! It's not up to you to get this plane home."

He looked at me as if I were crazy and told me to buzz off.

I so hope you won't. Some of you need to sit down. You fly furiously back and forth, ever busy, always thinking the success of this journey is up to you. Do you fear letting up?

Look out the windows. God's wings sustain you. God's engines empower you. You can flap like a fly and not accelerate this flight. It's your job to sit and trust: to receive.

Accept his power. You be the glove and let him get his hand deep into your life.

Surrender to his plan. Get rid of those cable-nibbling varmints.

And *keep* at it. Unceasingly seek God's Spirit.

Accept. Surrender. Keep at it. A-S-K. "Your Heavenly Father will give the Holy Spirit to those who ask him!" (Luke 11:13 PHILLIPS).

NINE

It's Not Up to You

Why anyone would pester Hannah Lake is beyond me. If the sweet face of this ten-year-old doesn't de-starch your shirt, her cherubic voice will. But, according to her dad, a grade school bully tried to stir some trouble. Intimidation tactics, pressure—the pest tried it all. But Hannah didn't fold. And in the end, it was not her dimples or tender voice but her faith that pulled her through.

The older student warned Hannah to prepare for battle. "Any day now I'm coming after you." Hannah didn't flinch or cry. She simply informed the perpetrator about the facts. "Do whatever you need to do," she explained. "But just know this: God is on my side."

Last word has it that no more threats have been made.

Elementary school bullies don't await you, but funeral homes do. Job transfers and fair-weather friends do. Challenges pockmark the pathway of your life. Where do you find energy to face them? God never promises an absence of distress. But he does promise the assuring presence of his Holy Spirit.

At first blush, a person might assume that the Holy Spirit is all about the spectacular and stupendous. We've seen the television images of sweating preachers, fainting and falling audiences, unintelligible tongue speaking, and questionable miracle working. While no one would deny the pupil-popping nature of the Holy Spirit's work (tongues of fire over the apostles' heads), a focus on the phenomenal might lead you to miss his quieter stabilizing work.

The Holy Spirit invisibly, yet indispensably, serves as a rudder for the ship of your soul, keeping you afloat and on track. This is no solo journey. Next time you feel as though it is, review some of the gifts the Spirit gives. For example, "you were sealed in Him with the Holy Spirit of promise, who is given as a pledge of our inheritance" (Eph. 1:13–14 NASB).

The Spirit seals you. The verb *sealed* stirs a variety of images. To protect a letter, you seal the envelope. To keep air out of a jar, you seal its mouth with a rubber-ringed lid. To keep oxygen from the wine, you seal the opening with cork and wax. To seal a deal, you might sign a contract or notarize a signature. Sealing declares ownership and secures contents.

The most famous New Testament "sealing" occurred with the tomb of Jesus. Roman soldiers rolled a rock over the entrance and "set a seal on the stone" (Matt. 27:66 NASB). Archaeologists envision two ribbons stretched in front of the entrance, glued together with hardened wax that bore the imprimatur of the Roman government—SPQR (*Senatus Populusque Romanus*)—as if to say, "Stay away! The contents of this tomb belong to Rome." Their seal, of course, proved futile.

The seal of the Spirit, however, proves forceful. When you accepted Christ, God sealed you with the Spirit. "Having believed, you were marked in him with a seal, the promised Holy Spirit" (Eph. 1:13 NIV). When hell's interlopers come seeking to snatch you from God, the seal turns them away. He bought you, owns you, and protects you. God paid too high a price to leave you unguarded. As Paul writes later, "Remember, he is the one who has identified you as his own, guaranteeing that you will be saved on the day of redemption" (Eph. 4:30).

In his delightful book *The Dance of Hope,* my friend Bill Frey tells of a blind student named John, whom he tutored at the University of Colorado in 1951. One day Bill asked John how he had become blind. The sightless student described an accident that had happened in his teenage years. The tragedy took not just the boy's sight but also his hope. He told Bill, "I was bitter and angry with God for letting it happen, and I took my anger out on everyone around me. I felt that since I had no future, I wouldn't lift a finger on my own behalf. Let others wait on me. I shut my bedroom door and refused to come out except for meals."

His admission surprised Bill. The student he assisted displayed no bitterness or anger. He asked John to explain the change. John credited his father. Weary of the pity party and ready for his son to get on with life, he reminded the boy of the impending winter and told him to mount the storm windows. "Do the work before I get home or else," the dad insisted, slamming the door on the way out.

John reacted with anger. Muttering and cursing and groping all the way to the garage, he found the windows, stepladder, and tools and went to work. "They'll be sorry when I fall off my ladder and break my neck." But he didn't fall. Little by little he inched around the house and finished the chore.

The assignment achieved the dad's goal. John reluctantly realized he could still work and began to reconstruct his life. Years later he learned something else about that day. When he shared this detail with Bill, his blind eyes misted. "I later discovered that at no time during the day had my father ever been more than four or five feet from my side."[1]

The father had no intention of letting the boy fall.

Your Father has no intention of letting you fall, either. You can't see him, but he is present. You are "shielded by God's power" (1 Pet. 1:5 NIV). He is "able to keep you from falling and to present you before his glorious presence without fault and with great joy" (Jude 24 NIV).

Drink deeply from this truth. God is able to keep you from falling! Does he want you living in fear? No! Just the opposite. "The Spirit we received does not make us slaves again to fear; it makes us children of God. With that Spirit we cry out, 'Father.' And the Spirit himself joins with our spirits to say we are God's children" (Rom. 8:15–16 NCV).

What an intriguing statement. Deep within you, God's Spirit confirms with your spirit that you belong to him. Beneath the vitals of the heart, God's Spirit whispers, "You are mine. I bought you and sealed you, and no one can take you." The Spirit offers an inward, comforting witness.

He is like a father who walks hand in hand with his little child. The child knows he belongs to his daddy, his small hand happily lost in the large one. He feels no uncertainty about his papa's love. But suddenly the father, moved by some impulse, swings his boy up into the air and into his arms and says, "I love you, Son." He puts a big kiss on the bubbly cheek, lowers the boy to the ground, and the two go on walking together.

Has the relationship between the two changed? On one level, no. The father is no more the father than he was before the expression of love. But on a deeper level, yes. The dad drenched, showered, and saturated the boy in love. God's Spirit does the same with us. "The love of God has been poured out in our hearts by the Holy Spirit who was given to us" (Rom. 5:5 NKJV). Note the preposition *of*. The Holy Spirit pours the love *of* God in our hearts, not love *for* God. God hands a bucket of love to the Spirit and instructs, "Douse their hearts."

There are moments when the Spirit enchants us with sweet rhapsody. *You belong to the Father. Signed, sealed, and soon-to-be delivered.* Been a while since you heard him whisper words of assurance? Then tell him. He's listening to you. And—get this!— he's speaking for you.

> The Spirit comes to the aid of our weakness. We do not even know how we ought to pray, but through our inarticulate groans the Spirit himself is pleading for us, and God who searches our inmost being knows what the Spirit means, because he pleads for God's own people in God's own way. (Rom. 8:26–27 NEB)

The Spirit comes to the aid of our weakness. What a sentence worthy of a highlighter. Who does not need this reminder? Weak bodies. Weak wills. Weakened resolves. We've known them all. The word *weakness* can refer to physical infirmities, as with the invalid who had been unable to walk for thirty-eight years (John 5:5), or spiritual impotence, as with the spiritually "helpless" of Romans 5:6.

Whether we are feeble of soul or body or both, how good to know it's not up to us. "The Spirit himself is pleading for us."

I witnessed a picture of the strong speaking for the weak during a White House briefing on the AIDS crisis. While most of the attendees represented relief organizations, a few ministers were invited. The agenda of the day included a Q and A with a White House staffer charged with partial oversight of several billion dollars earmarked for AIDS prevention and treatment. There were many questions. How does one qualify? How much can an organization hope to receive? What are the requirements, if any, for using the moneys? Most of the questions came from organizations. Most of us ministers were silent.

But not Bob Coy. Bob serves a large congregation in Fort Lauderdale, Florida. From earlier conversations, I knew of his heart for AIDS victims. When he raised his hand, I expected a policy question. Wrong. He had a personal question. "One of my friends in Miami is dying from AIDS. He spends two thousand dollars a month on medication. With insurance balking at coverage, I'm wondering if I might find him some assistance."

The White House policy staffer was surprised, but polite. "Uh, sure. After the meeting I'll put you in touch with the right person."

The minister, determined to bring the problem to the top of the food chain, remained standing. He held up a few sheets of stapled paper. "I brought his documents with me. If more is needed, I can run them down."

The government official remained polite. "Absolutely. After the meeting."

He had fielded another question or two when he noticed the minister from Florida had raised his hand again. This time the preacher went to the bottom line. "I'm still thinking of my friend," he explained. "Who signs the checks?"

"Excuse me?"

"Who signs the checks? I just want to talk to the person who makes the decisions. So I want to know, who signs the checks?"

My initial response was, *What audacity!* The minister seizing a White House moment to help a friend. Then I thought, *What loyalty! Does the bedridden friend in Florida have any idea that his cause is being presented a few hundred feet from the Oval Office?*

Do you have any idea that your needs are being described in heaven? The Holy Spirit "prays for us with groanings that cannot be expressed in words. And the Father who knows all hearts knows what the Spirit is saying, for the Spirit pleads for us believers in harmony with God's own will" (Rom. 8:26–27).

The AIDS-infected man has no voice, no clout, and no influence. But he has a friend. And his friend speaks on his behalf. The impoverished orphan of Russia, the distraught widow of the battle-field, the aging saint in the convalescent home—they may think they have no voice, no clout, no influence. But they have a friend—a counselor, a comforter—the blessed Spirit of God, who speaks the language of heaven in heaven. "He does our praying in and for us, making prayer out of our wordless sighs, our aching groans. He . . . keeps us present before God" (vv. 26–27 MSG).

It's not up to you to pray your prayers. None of us pray as much as we should, but all of us pray more than we think, because the Holy Spirit turns our sighs into petitions and tears into entreaties. He speaks for you and protects you. He makes sure you get heard. He makes sure you get home.

Now, suppose a person never hears this, never learns about the sealing and intercession of the Spirit. This individual thinks that salvation security resides in self, not God, that prayer power depends on the person, not the Spirit. What kind of life will this person lead?

A parched and prayerless one. Fighting to stay spiritually afloat drains him. Thinking he stands alone before God discourages him. So he lives parched and prayerless.

But what about the one who believes in the work of the Spirit? Really believes. Suppose a person drinks from this fountain? Better still, suppose you do. Suppose you let the Spirit saturate you with assurance. After all, "we can't round up enough containers to hold everything God generously pours into our lives through the Holy Spirit!" (Rom. 5:5 MSG).

Will you be different as a result? You bet your sweet Sunday you will. Your shoulders will lift as you lower the buckling weight of self-salvation. Your knees will bend as you discover the buoyant power of the praying Spirit. Higher walk. Deeper prayers. And, most of all, a quiet confidence that comes from knowing it's not up to you. And you, like Hannah, can tell the pests of the world, "Do whatever you need to do. But just know this: God is on my side."

Part Three

Trust His

Lordship

TEN

In God We (Nearly) Trust

A few days before our wedding, Denalyn and I enjoyed and endured a sailing voyage. Milt, a Miami church friend, had invited Denalyn, her mom, and me to join him and a few others on a leisurely cruise along the Florida coast.

Initially it was just that. Leisure. We stretched out on cushions, hung feet over the side, caught some zzz's and rays. Nice.

But then came the storm. The sky darkened, the rain started, and the flat ocean humped like a dragon's neck. Sudden waves of water tilted the vessel up until we saw nothing but sky and then downward until we saw nothing but blue. I learned this about sailing: there is nothing swell about a swell. Tanning stopped. Napping ceased. Eyes turned first to the thunderclouds, then to the captain. We looked to Milt.

He was deliberate and decisive. He told some people where to sit, others what to do, and all of us to hang on. And we did what he said. Why? We knew he knew best. No one else knew the difference between starboard and stern. Only Milt did. We trusted him. We knew he knew.

And we knew we didn't. Prior to the winds, we might have boasted about Boy Scout merit badges in sailing or bass-boat excursions. But once the storm hit, we shut up. (Except for Denalyn, who threw up.) We had no choice but to trust Milt. He knew what we didn't—and he cared. The vessel was captained, not by a hireling or a stranger, but by a pal. Our safety mattered to him. So we trusted him.

Oh, that the choice were equally easy in life. Need I remind you about your westerly winds? With the speed of lightning and the force of a thunderclap, williwaws anger tranquil waters. Victims of sudden storms populate unemployment lines and ICU wards. You know the winds. You've felt the waves. Good-bye, smooth sailing. Hello, rough waters.

Such typhoons test our trust in the Captain. Does God know what he is doing? Can he get us out? Why did he allow the storm? The conditions worsen, and his instructions perplex: he calls on you to endure disaster, tolerate criticism, forgive an enemy . . . How do you respond?

Can you say about God what I said about Milt?

I know God knows what's best.

I know I don't.

I know he cares.

Such words come easily when the water is calm. But when you're looking at a wrecked car or a suspicious-looking mole, when war breaks out or thieves break in, do you trust him?

If yes, then you're scoring high marks in the classroom of sovereignty. This important biblical phrase defines itself. Zero in on the middle portion of the term. See the word within the word?

Sove-*reign*-ty. To confess the sovereignty of God is to acknowledge the reign of God, his regal authority and veto power over everything that happens. To embrace God's sovereignty is to drink from the well of his lordship and make a sailboat-in-the-storm decision. Not in regard to Milt and the sea, but in regard to God and life. You look toward the Captain and resolve: he knows what's best.

After all, doesn't he quarterback the activities of the universe?

> For our God is in the heavens,
>
> and he does as he wishes.
>
> (Ps. 115:3)

From eternity to eternity I am God. No one can oppose what I do. No one can reverse my actions. (Isa. 43:13)

Only I can tell you what is going to happen even before it happens. Everything I plan will come to pass, for I do whatever I wish. (Isa. 46:10)

He chose us from the beginning, and all things happen just as he decided long ago. (Eph. 1:11)

Divine decrees direct the cosmos. Jesus informed Pilate, "You would have no power over me if it were not given to you from above" (John 19:11 NIV). The Jewish leaders thought they were the ones who sent Christ to the cross. Peter corrected them. Jesus was "delivered over by the predetermined plan and foreknowledge of God" (Acts 2:23 NASB).

Jeremiah rhetorically inquired, "Can anything happen without the Lord's permission?" (Lam. 3:37).

The book of Daniel declares no! "[God] has the power to do as he pleases among the angels of heaven and with those who live on earth. No one can stop him or challenge him, saying, 'What do you mean by doing these things?'" (Dan. 4:35).

Scripture, from Old Testament to New, from prophets to poets to preachers, renders one unanimous chorus: God directs the affairs of humanity. As Paul wrote, "God . . . is the *blessed controller* of all things, the king over all kings and the master of all masters" (1 Tim. 6:15 PHILLIPS, emphasis mine).

No leaf falls without God's knowledge. No dolphin gives birth without his permission. No wave crashes on the shore apart from his calculation. God has never been surprised. Not once. "The Son is . . . sustaining all things by his powerful word" (Heb. 1:3 NIV). "He himself gives life and breath to everything, and he satisfies every need there is" (Acts 17:25). King David proclaimed, "In Your book were written all the days that were ordained for me, when as yet there was not one of them" (Ps. 139:16 NASB).

Denying the sovereignty of God requires busy scissors and results in a hole-y Bible, for many holes are made as the verses are cut out. Amazingly, some people opt to extract such passages. Unable to reconcile human suffering with absolute sovereignty, they dilute God's Word. Rabbi Kushner did.

His book *When Bad Things Happen to Good People* reached a disturbing conclusion: God can't run the world. Kushner suggested that Job, the most famous sufferer, was "forced to choose between a good God who is not totally powerful, or a powerful God who is not totally good."[1]

The rabbi speaks for many. *God is strong. Or God is good. But God is not both.* Else, how do you explain birth defects, coast-crashing hurricanes, AIDS, or the genocide of the Tutsi in the 1990s? If God cares, he isn't strong; if he is strong, he doesn't care. He can't be both.

But according to the Bible, he is exactly that. Furthermore, according to the Bible, the problem is not the strength or kindness of God. The problem is the agenda of the human race. We pursue the wrong priority. We want good health, a good income, a good night's rest, and a good retirement. Our priority is *We*.

God's priority, however, is God. Why do the heavens exist? To flaunt God. "The heavens declare the glory of God" (Ps. 19:1 NIV).

Why do people struggle? To display his strength. "I have tested you in the furnace of affliction. For My own sake, for My own sake, I will act" (Isa. 48:10–11 NASB). The prophet proclaimed, "You lead Your people, to make Yourself a glorious name" (Isa. 63:14 NKJV).

God unfurls his own flag. He flexes his own muscles. Heaven does not ask, "How can I make Max happy?" Heaven asks, "How can I use Max to reveal my excellencies?" He may use blessings. Then again, he may use buffetings. Both belong to him.

> I am the one who creates the light and makes the darkness. I am the one who sends good times and bad times. I, the LORD, am the one who does these things. (Isa. 45:7)

> Enjoy prosperity while you can. But when hard times strike, realize that both come from God. (Eccles. 7:14)

> Is it not from the mouth of the Most High
> That woe and well-being proceed?
> (Lam. 3:38 NKJV)

Sometime ago I went to the Indianapolis airport to catch a return flight to San Antonio. Upon reaching the terminal, I realized I had lost my itinerary. But that was okay, because I knew which airline would carry me home. Continental. Having flown from San Antonio on Continental, I would return on Continental. Right? But the Continental counter was closed. The lights were off. No ticket agent was in sight. With the clock ticking toward my 7:40 p.m. departure, I called for help. "Hello? Anyone back there? I'm here for the 7:40 flight."

From within the catacombs emerged a Continental baggage handler. He looked at me and said, "We don't have a 7:40 flight."

I replied, "Yes, you do. I flew Continental here, and I need to fly it home."

He shrugged. "We don't have another flight tonight."

I turned to the automated ticket machine, entered my information, and requested a boarding pass for the 7:40 flight. It informed me that there was no such thing. Wouldn't you know? Even the machine was wrong!

The employee, much to his credit, bore with me. Scratching his bald head, he offered a solution. "You know, Northwest Airlines has a 7:40 flight. Maybe you should check with them."

Sure enough, they did. And I had to admit that the airline's schedule ranked higher than my opinion. Their authority checkmated mine. I could have stood in front of the Continental counter all night, stamping my feet and demanding my way. But what good would it have done? Eventually I had to submit to the truth of the itinerary.

Every so often in life, we find ourselves standing before God's counter, thinking we know the itinerary. Good health, a job promotion, a pregnancy. Many times God checks the itinerary he created and says yes. But there are times when he says, "No. That isn't the journey I have planned for you. I have you routed through the city of Struggle."

We can stamp our feet and shake our fists. Or we can make a sailor-in-the-storm decision. *I know God knows what is best.*

Some find the thought impossible to accept. One dear woman did. After I shared these ideas in a public setting, she asked to speak with me. Husband at her side, she related the story of her horrible childhood. First abused, then abandoned by her father. Unimaginable and undeserved hurts scar her early memories. Through tear-filled eyes she asked, "Do you mean to tell me God was watching the whole time?"

The question vibrated in the room. I shifted in my chair and answered, "Yes, he was. I don't know why he allowed your abuse, but I do know this. He loves you and hurts with you." She didn't like the answer. But dare we say anything else? Dare we suggest that God dozed off? Abandoned his post? That heaven sees but can't act? That our Father is kind but not strong, or strong but doesn't care?

I wish she could have spoken to Joseph. His brothers abused him, selling him into slavery. Was God watching? Yes. And our sovereign God used their rebellious hearts to save a nation from famine and the family of the Messiah from extinction. As Joseph told them, "God turned into good what you meant for evil" (Gen. 50:20).

I wish she could have spoken to Lazarus. He grew deathly ill. When Jesus heard the news, he did nothing. Jesus waited until Lazarus was four-days dead in the grave. Why? "For the glory of God, so that the Son of God may be glorified by it" (John 11:4 NASB).

Best of all would have been a conversation with Jesus himself. He begged God for a different itinerary: a crossless death. From Gethsemane's garden Christ pleaded for a plan B. Redemption with no nails. " 'Father, if you are willing, please take this cup of suffering away from me. Yet I want your will, not mine.' Then an angel from heaven appeared and strengthened him" (Luke 22:42–43).

Did God hear the prayer of his Son? Enough to send an angel. Did God spare his Son from death? No. The glory of God outranked the comfort of Christ. So Christ suffered, and God's grace was displayed and deployed.

Are you called to endure a Gethsemane season? Have you "been granted for Christ's sake, not only to believe in Him, but also to suffer for His sake" (Phil. 1:29 NASB)?

If so, then come thirsty and drink deeply from his lordship. He authors all itineraries. He knows what is best. No struggle will come your way apart from his purpose, presence, and permission. What encouragement this brings! You are never the victim of nature or the prey of fate. Chance is eliminated. You are more than a weather vane whipped about by the winds of fortune. Would God truly abandon you to the whims of drug-crazed thieves, greedy corporate raiders, or evil leaders? Perish the thought!

> When you pass through the waters, I will be with you;
> And through the rivers, they will not overflow you.
> When you walk through the fire, you will not be scorched,
> Nor will the flame burn you.
> For I am the LORD your God.
> (Isa. 43:2–3 NASB)

We live beneath the protective palm of a sovereign King who superintends every circumstance of our lives and delights in doing us good.

Nothing comes your way that has not first passed through the filter of his love. Margaret Clarkson, in her wonderfully titled book *Grace Grows Best in Winter,* wrote:

> The sovereignty of God is the one impregnable rock to which the suffering human heart must cling. The circumstances surrounding our lives are no accident: they may be the work of evil, but that evil is held firmly within the mighty hand of our sovereign God. . . . All evil is subject to Him, and evil cannot touch His children unless He permits it. God is the Lord of human history and the personal history of every member of his redeemed family.[2]

Learn well the song of sovereignty: *I know God knows what's best.* Pray humbly the prayer of trust: "I trust your lordship. I belong to you. Nothing comes to me that hasn't passed through you."

A word of caution: the doctrine of sovereignty challenges us. Study it gradually. Don't share it capriciously. When someone you love faces adversity, don't insensitively declare, "God is in control." A cavalier tone can eclipse the right truth. Be careful.

And be encouraged. God's ways are always right. They may not make sense to us. They may be mysterious, inexplicable, difficult, and even painful. But they are right. "And we know that God causes everything to work together for the good of those who love God and are called according to his purpose for them" (Rom. 8:28).

As John Oxenham wrote in 1913:

GOD'S HANDWRITING

He writes in characters too grand
For our short sight to understand;
We catch but broken strokes, and try
To fathom all the mystery
Of withered hopes, of death, of life,
The endless war, the useless strife,—
But there, with larger, clearer sight,
We shall see this—His way was right.[3]

ELEVEN

Worry?
You Don't Have To

The idea captured the fancy of futuristic scientists: an eight-story, glass-and-steel dome in which eight scientists could lead a self-sustained life. The outside elements of the Sonora Desert would not touch them. Let the sun blaze. Let the winds blow. Let the sand fly. Safe within the dome the researchers would be untouched.

So, with the hope of developing a space-colony prototype, the biospherians entered the two-hundred-million-dollar, three-acre terrarium in 1991.[1] They planted their seeds and grew their food; scientists watched with fascination, and not too few of us felt a tinge of envy.

Who hasn't longed for a rotunda of relief? Not from an Arizona desert, but from the harsh winds and hot sun of life. The bank demands the mortgage each month. Hospital bills pack a knockout punch. Semester finals lurk around the corner.

And look around you. You have reason to worry. The sun blasts cancer-causing rays. Air vents blow lung-clotting molds. Potato chips have too many carbs. Vegetables, too many toxins. And do they have to call an airport a terminal? Why does the pilot tell passengers, "We are about to make our *final* approach"? Even on the ground, the flight attendant urges us to stay seated until we have reached a "complete stop." Is there any other kind? Do some airlines have "sort of stops," "partial stops," or "little bits of stops"?

Some of us have postgraduate degrees from the University of Anxiety. We go to sleep worried that we won't wake up; we wake up worried that we didn't sleep. We worry that someone will discover that lettuce was fattening all along. The mother of one teenager bemoaned, "My daughter doesn't tell me anything. I'm a nervous wreck." Another mother replied, "My daughter tells me everything. I'm a nervous wreck." Wouldn't you love to stop worrying? Could you use a strong shelter from life's harsh elements?

God offers you just that: the possibility of a worry-free life. Not just less worry, but no worry. He created a dome for your heart. "His peace will guard your hearts and minds as you live in Christ Jesus" (Phil. 4:7).

Interested? Then take a good look at the rest of the passage.

Don't worry about anything; instead, pray about everything. Tell God what you need, and thank him for all he has done. If you do this, you will experience God's peace, which is far more wonderful than the human mind can understand. His peace will guard your hearts and minds as you live in Christ Jesus. (vv. 6–7)

The Christians in Philippi needed a biosphere. Attacks were coming at them from all angles. Preachers served for selfish gain (1:15–17). Squabbling church members threatened the unity of the church (4:2). False teachers preached a crossless gospel (3:2–3, 18–19). Some believers struggled to find food and shelter (4:19). Persecutions outside. Problems inside.

Enough hornets' nests to make you worry. Folks in Philippi had them. Folks today have them. To them and us God gives the staggering proposal: "Don't worry about anything."

Yeah, right. And while I'm at it, I'll leapfrog the moon. Are you kidding?

Jesus isn't. Two words summarize his opinion of worry: *irrelevant* and *irreverent*.

"Can all your worries add a single moment to your life? Of course not" (Matt. 6:27). Worry is irrelevant. It alters nothing. When was the last time you solved a problem by worrying about it? Imagine someone saying, "I got behind in my bills, so I resolved to worry my way out of debt. And, you know, it worked! A few sleepless nights, a day of puking and hand wringing. I yelled at my kids and took some pills, and—glory to worry—money appeared on my desk."

It doesn't happen! Worry changes nothing. You don't add one day to your life or one bit of life to your day by worrying. Your anxiety earns you heartburn, nothing more. Regarding the things about which we fret:

- 40 percent never happen
- 30 percent regard unchangeable deeds of the past
- 12 percent focus on the opinions of others that cannot be controlled
- 10 percent center on personal health, which only worsens as we worry about it
- 8 percent concern real problems that we can influence[2]

Ninety-two percent of our worries are needless! Not only is worry irrelevant, doing nothing; worry is irreverent, distrusting God.

> And why worry about your clothes? Look at the lilies and how they grow. They don't work or make their clothing, yet Solomon in all his glory was not dressed as beautifully as they are. And if God cares so wonderfully for flowers that are here today and gone tomorrow, won't he more surely care for you? *You have so little faith!* (Matt. 6:28–30, emphasis mine)

Worry betrays a fragile faith, an "unconscious blasphemy."[3] We don't intentionally doubt God, but don't we, when we worry, essentially doubt God? We assume the attitude of a kid asking Michelangelo, "You sure you know what to do with that rock?" No wonder the apostle urges us to "be anxious for nothing" (Phil. 4:6 NASB). Paul is not promoting an irresponsible, careless life. We are not to be like the procrastinating minister. *I won't worry,* he told himself. *The Holy Spirit will give me my message.* All week long he avoided his work, saying, *The Holy Spirit will give me my message.* Finally, on Sunday, he stood before the church and prayed aloud, "All right, Lord. Give me a message." Much to the surprise of the church, a heavenly voice filled the sanctuary. "Tell the people you didn't study."

Manage your problems? Of course. But let your problems manage you? The worrisome heart does.

And the worrisome heart pays a high price for doing so. *Worry* comes from the Greek word that means "to divide the mind." Anxiety splits us right down the middle, creating a double-minded thinker. Rather than take away tomorrow's trouble, worry voids today's strength. Perception is divided, distorting your vision.

Strength is divided, wasting your energy. Who can afford to lose power?

But how can we stop doing so? Paul offers a two-pronged answer: God's part and our part. Our part includes prayer and gratitude. "Don't worry about anything; instead, *pray* about everything. Tell God what you need, and *thank him* for all he has done" (Phil. 4:6, emphasis mine).

Want to worry less? Then pray more. Rather than look forward in fear, look upward in faith. This command surprises no one. Regarding prayer, the Bible never blushes. Jesus taught people that "it was necessary for them to pray consistently and never quit" (Luke 18:1 MSG). Paul told believers, "Devote yourselves to prayer with an alert mind and a thankful heart" (Col. 4:2). James declared, "Are any among you suffering? They should keep on praying about it" (James 5:13).

Rather than worry about anything, "pray about everything." Everything? Diaper changes and dates? Business meetings and broken bathtubs? Procrastinations and prognostications? Pray about everything. "In everything . . . let your requests be made known to God" (Phil. 4:6 NKJV).

When we lived in Rio de Janeiro, Brazil, I used to take my daughters on bus rides. For a few pennies, we could board a bus and ride all over the city. May sound dull to us, but if you are two years old, such a day generates World Cup excitement. The girls did nothing on the trip. I bought the token, carried the backpack, and selected the route. My only request of them was this: "Stay close to me." Why? I knew the kind of characters who might board a bus. And God forbid that my daughters and I got separated.

Our Father makes the same request. "Stay close to me. Talk to me. Pray to me. Breathe me in and exhale your worry." Worry diminishes as we look upward. God knows what can happen on this journey, and he wants to bring us home.

Pray about everything.

And don't skip Paul's ingredient of gratitude. "Tell God what you need, and thank him for all he has done."

Do what the shepherd boy David did when he faced Goliath. David didn't cower before the giant's strength. He focused on God's success. When Saul refused to let him go head to knee with Goliath, David produced God's track record.

"I have been taking care of my father's sheep," he said. "When a lion or a bear comes to steal a lamb from the flock, I go after it with a club and take the lamb from its mouth. If the animal turns on me, I catch it by the jaw and club it to death. I have done this to both lions and bears, and I'll do it to this pagan Philistine, too, for he has defied the armies of the living God! The LORD who saved me from the claws of the lion and the bear will save me from this Philistine!"

Saul finally consented. "All right, go ahead," he said. "And may the LORD be with you!" (1 Sam. 17:34–37)

Are you afraid of a giant? Then recall the lion and the bear. Don't look forward in fear; look backward in appreciation. God's proof is God's past. Forgetfulness sires fearfulness, but a good memory makes for a good heart.

It works like this. Let's say a stress stirrer comes your way. The doctor decides you need an operation. She detects a lump and thinks it best that you have it removed. So there you are, walking out of her office. You've just been handed this cup of anxiety. What are you going to do with it? You can place it in one of two pots.

You can dump your bad news in the vat of worry and pull out the spoon. Turn on the fire. Stew on it. Stir it. Mope for a while. Brood for a time. Won't be long before you'll have a delightful pot of pessimism. Some of you have been sipping from this vat for a long time. Your friends and family have asked me to tell you that the stuff you're drinking is getting to you.

How about a different idea? The pot of prayer. Before the door of the doctor's office closes, give the problem to God. "I receive your lordship. Nothing comes to me that hasn't passed through you." In addition, stir in a healthy helping of gratitude. You don't think about a lion and bear, but you do remember the tax refund, the timely counsel, or the suddenly open seat on the overbooked flight. A glimpse into the past generates strength for the future.

Your part is prayer and gratitude.

God's part? Peace and protection. "If you do this, you will experience God's peace, which is far more wonderful than the human mind can understand. His peace will guard your hearts and minds as you live in Christ Jesus" (Phil. 4:7).

Believing prayer ushers in God's peace. Not a random, nebulous, earthly peace, but his peace. Imported from heaven. The same tranquillity that marks the throne room, God offers to you.

Do you think he battles anxiety? You suppose he ever wrings his hands or asks the angels for antacids? Of course not. A problem is no more a challenge to God than a twig is to an elephant. God enjoys perfect peace because God enjoys perfect power.

And he offers his peace to you. A peace that will "guard your hearts and minds as you live in Christ Jesus." Paul employs a military metaphor here. The Philippians, living in a garrison town, were accustomed to the Roman sentries maintaining their watch. Before any enemy could get inside, he had to pass through the guards. God gives you the same offer. His supernatural peace overshadows you like a protective dome, guarding your heart.

After twenty-four months, the biosphere in Arizona proved to be a total flop. Biological balance between the plants got out of whack. Oxygen dipped dangerously low. Researchers squabbled among themselves. The ants ran amuck and conquered most of the other bugs. The experiment failed, and the dome was abandoned.

But the dome of God still stands. We need only stay beneath it. Are you tied up in knots? "Cast all your anxiety on him because he cares for you" (1 Pet. 5:7 NIV). Strong verb there. *Cast*. Not *place, lay,* or *occasionally offer*. Peter enlisted the same verb Gospel writers used to describe the way Jesus treated demons. He cast them out. An authoritative hand on the collar, another on the belt, and a "Don't come back." Do the same with your fears. Get serious with them. Immediately cast them upon God.

Worry is an option, not an assignment. God can lead you into a worry-free world. Be quick to pray. Focus less on the problems ahead and more on the victories behind. Do your part, and God will do his. He will guard your heart with his peace . . . a peace that passes understanding.

TWELVE

Angels Watching over You

When seventeen-year-old Jake Porter ran onto the football field, both teams cheered. Odd that they would. In three years on the Northwest High squad, he'd barely dirtied a game jersey. The McDermott, Ohio, fans had never seen Jake carry the ball or make a tackle. Nor had they seen him read a book or write much more than a sentence. Kids with chromosomal fragile X syndrome, a common cause of mental retardation, seldom do.

But Jake loved sports. Each day after his special-ed classes, he dashed off to some practice: track, baseball, basketball. Never missed. Never played, either.

Until the Waverly game.

Jake's coach made his decision before the kickoff. If a lopsided score rendered the final seconds superfluous, Jake would come in. The lopsided part proved true. With five ticks remaining on the clock, his team was down 42–0. So the coach called a time-out.

He motioned to speak with the opposing coach. As his Waverly counterpart heard the plan, he began shaking his head and waving his hands. He disagreed with something. A referee intervened, and play resumed.

The quarterback took the ball and handed it to Jake. Jake knew what do: take a knee and let the clock expire. They'd practiced this play all week. But, to his surprise, the players wouldn't let him. His teammates told him to run. So he did. In the wrong direction. So the back judge stopped and turned him around.

That's when the Waverly defense did their part. The visiting coach, as it turns out, wasn't objecting to the play. He was happy for Porter to carry the ball but not for him just to run out the clock. He wanted Jake to score. Waverly players parted like the Red Sea for Moses and shouted for Jake to run. Run he did. Grinning and dancing and jumping all the way to the end zone.

Both sidelines celebrated. Moms cried, cheerleaders whooped, and Jake smiled as if he'd won the lottery without buying a ticket.[1]

How often do such things happen? According to the Bible, more often than you might think. In fact, what Jake's team did for him, the Lord of the universe does for you every day of your life. And you ought to see the team he coaches.

> The angels keep their ancient places—
> Turn but a stone and start a wing!
> 'Tis ye, 'tis your estrangéd faces,
> That miss the many-splendored thing.[2]

Has your face missed the angels? With over three hundred scriptural references, these celestial servants occupy an unquestioned role in the Bible. If you believe in God's Word, you have to believe in angels. At the same time, you have to be puzzled by them. Angel study is biblical whale watching. Angels surface just long enough to grant a glimpse and raise a question but then disappear before we have a full view.

One thing is certain: biblical and contemporary portrayals of angels don't match up. Grocery store tabloids present angels as Thumbelina fairies with see-through wings. They exist to do us favors—heaven's version of bottled genies who find parking places, lost keys, and missing cats. Snap your finger and "poof," they appear. Snap again and they vanish.

Not quite a biblical image. Two adjectives capture the greater truth about angels: *many* and *mighty*.

Multitudes of angels populate the world. Hebrews 12:22 speaks of "thousands of angels in joyful assembly." Jude declared, "The Lord is coming with thousands and thousands of holy angels to judge everyone" (vv. 14–15 CEV). An inspired King David wrote, "The chariots of God are twenty thousand, even thousands of angels: the Lord is among them, as in Sinai, in the holy place" (Ps. 68:17 KJV). When referring to Mt. Sinai, David was thinking of the time ten thousand angels descended on the mountain as God gave the law to Moses. "GOD came down from Sinai . . . coming with ten thousand holy angels" (Deut. 33:2 MSG).

Thousands of angels awaited the call of Christ on the day of the cross. "Do you think that I cannot appeal to My Father, and He will at once put at My disposal more than twelve legions of angels?" (Matt. 26:53 NASB). One legion equated to six thousand soldiers. Quick math reveals that seventy-two thousand hosts of heaven (enough to fill Los Angeles's Angel Stadium more than one and a half times) stood poised to rescue their Master. The book of Revelation, brimming as it is with glimpses into the soon-to-be world, refers to angels around the heavenly throne, "and the number of them was ten thousand times ten thousand, and thousands of thousands" (Rev. 5:11 NKJV).

And don't forget the vision given to Elisha's servant. When an army threatened to take the lives of them both, Elisha asked God to open the eyes of the boy. "Then the LORD opened the eyes of the young man, and he saw. And behold, the mountain was full of horses and chariots of fire all around Elisha" (2 Kings 6:17 NKJV).

If God opened our eyes, what would we see? Moms and dads, you'd see angels escorting your child to school. Travelers, you'd see angels encircling the aircraft. Patients, you'd see angels monitoring the moves of the surgeon. Teenagers, you'd see angels overseeing your sleep. Many, many angels. Hundreds of years ago John Milton wrote, "Millions of spiritual creatures walk the Earth unseen, both when we wake, and when we sleep."[3]

The poet was right: "Turn but a stone and start a wing."

You need an adjective to describe angels? Start with *many*.

Continue with *mighty*. Chiffon wings and meringue sweetness? Perhaps for angels in the gift books and specialty shops, but God's angels are marked by indescribable strength. Paul says Christ "will come with his mighty angels" (2 Thess. 1:7). From the word translated *mighty*, we have the English word *dynamic*. Angels pack dynamic force. It took only one angel to slay the firstborn of Egypt and only one angel to close the mouths of the lions to protect Daniel. David called angels "mighty creatures who carry out his plans, listening for each of his commands" (Ps. 103:20).

No need for you to talk to angels; they won't listen. Their ears incline only to God's voice. They are "spirits who serve God" (Heb. 1:14 NCV), responding to his command and following only his directions. Jesus said they "always see the face of my Father in heaven" (Matt. 18:10 NIV). Only one sound matters to angels—

God's voice. Only one sight enthralls angels—God's face. They know that he is Lord of all.

And as a result, they worship him. Whether in the temple with Isaiah or the pasture with the Bethlehem shepherds, angels worship. "When he presented his honored Son to the world, God said, 'Let all the angels of God worship him'" (Heb. 1:6). They did and they do.

Remember the earlier reference to the ten thousand times ten thousand angels encircling the throne of heaven? Guess what they are doing? "All the angels stood around the throne . . . saying: 'Amen! Blessing and glory and wisdom, thanksgiving and honor and power and might, be to our God forever and ever. Amen'" (Rev. 7:11–12 NKJV).

Doesn't their worship proclaim volumes about God's beauty? Angels could gaze at the Grand Tetons and Grand Canyon, Picasso paintings and the Sistine Chapel, but they choose, instead, to fix their eyes on the glory of God. They can't see enough of him, and they can't be silent about what they see.

At the very moment you read these words, God's sinless servants offer unceasing worship to their Maker. He is, remember, their creator. At one time no angels existed. And then, by God's decree, they did. "He made the things we can see and the things we can't see—kings, kingdoms, rulers, and authorities. Everything has been created through him and for him" (Col. 1:16). Angels fill God's invisible creation.

They worship him, and—here is a drink for thirsty hearts—they protect us. "All the angels are spirits who serve God and are sent to *help those who will receive salvation*" (Heb. 1:14 NCV, emphasis mine).

One of my friends recently took a heart-stopping mission trip to Vietnam. He and two companions set out to smuggle Bibles and money to Christians there. Upon landing, however, he was separated from the other two. He spoke no Vietnamese and had never traveled in Hanoi. Imagine his thoughts, then, as he stood in front of the airport, holding a bag of Bibles, wearing a belt of cash, and knowing nothing more than the name of his hotel.

Taxi driver after taxi driver offered his services, but he waited and prayed. Finally, knowing he needed to do something, he climbed into a taxi and spoke the name of the hotel. After an hour and a thousand turns, he found himself deposited at the designated place. He paid his drivers, and they went on their way.

That's right, "they" drove off. The front seat of his taxi had been occupied by two men. Only later did the uniqueness of this fact strike him. He saw hundreds of taxis during his days in Vietnam, but not another one of them had two drivers.

Meaningless detail? Quite possibly.

Affirming clue? Equally possible. Perhaps he was safely delivered, not by Vietnamese motorists, but by a tandem of heavenly couriers. His associates arrived but only after they'd been scammed by another taxi driver. Did God command a dynamic duo to protect my friend?

He certainly sent a powerful protector to Shadrach, Meshach, and Abednego. King Nebuchadnezzar commanded that the furnace fire be cranked up seven times its normal heat and that they be thrown into it. The king looked in, expecting to see a trio of misery; instead, the men were in fine company. A visitor stood next to them amid the flames. "'Look!' Nebuchadnezzar shouted. 'I see four men, unbound, walking around in the fire. They aren't even hurt by the flames! And the fourth looks like a divine being!'" (Dan. 3:25). An angel ministered to God's people.

And look at Peter, sleeping on a pallet in a Jerusalem prison's death row. One word from Herod and his head would roll. All earthly efforts to save him had expired. Heavenly efforts had not, however. An angel not only woke Peter up but also walked him out! The fisherman enjoyed a Jake Porter escort. "Suddenly, there was a bright light in the cell, and an angel of the Lord stood before Peter. The angel tapped him on the side to awaken him and said, 'Quick! Get up!' And the chains fell off his wrists" (Acts 12:7).

Angels minister to God's people. "[God] has put his angels in charge of you to watch over you wherever you go" (Ps. 91:11 NCV).

Billy Graham reminds us, "If you are a believer, expect powerful angels to accompany you in your life experience."[4] But what if you are not a believer? Do angels offer equal surveillance to God's enemies? No, they don't. The promise of angelic protection is limited to those who trust God. "All the angels are spirits who serve God and are sent to *help those who will receive salvation.*" David speaks of this restricted coverage: "For the angel of the LORD guards *all who fear him,* and he rescues them" (Ps. 34:7, emphasis mine). Refuse God at the risk of an unguarded back. But receive his lordship, and be assured that many mighty angels will guard you in all your ways.

"The angel of the LORD encamps all around those who fear Him, and delivers them" (v. 7 NKJV). He doesn't wave as he flies past; he encamps, he lingers, he keeps vigilance over you. You traffic beneath the care of celestial beings. Let that truth lower your anxiety level! The wealthiest of the world don't have the protection God's servants give you.

And angels love to give it! Angels not only serve you, they are stunned by you. "Do you realize how fortunate you are? Angels would have given anything to be in on this" (1 Pet. 1:12 MSG). Amazed angels behold the gifts God has given you. Does the Holy

Spirit indwell angels? No. But he dwells in you. Do angels thank God for salvation? No, they've never been lost. But you have. Did Christ become an angel? No. But he became a human. And angels stood in awe when he did. Worshiping angels attended his birth. Awaiting angels witnessed his death. Excited angels announced his resurrection. Attentive angels watch the work of the church. "Through Christians like yourselves gathered in churches, this extraordinary plan of God is becoming known and talked about even among the angels!" (Eph. 3:10 MSG).

God's work in you leaves angels wide-eyed and applauding. Jesus said, "There is joy in the presence of God's angels when even one sinner repents" (Luke 15:10). When angels gather in the break room for angel food cake, they discuss the church.

"Have you seen what is happening in Nigeria?"

"The Australians are taking great strides."

"Hey, I just returned from New York. Let me tell you about the Bronx believers."

The Hebrew writer describes a "great cloud of witnesses" (Heb. 12:1 NIV). Certainly angels are numbered among them.

God sends his best troops to oversee your life. Imagine the president assigning his Secret Service to protect you, telling his agents to motorcade your car through traffic and safeguard you through crowds. How would you sleep if you knew D.C.'s finest guarded your door? How *will* you sleep knowing heaven's finest are doing just that? You are not alone. Receive God's lordship over your life. Heaven's many, mighty angels watch over you.

And when you cross the goal line, they'll be the first to applaud.

THIRTEEN

With God as Your Guardian

Did I just read what I think I read? I drove around the block for a second glance. The announcement, taped to a stop-sign pole, had a home computer look to it: yellow paper and thick letters. Our neighbors, like yours, print and post all types of fliers. The presence of the announcement didn't surprise me, but the words did.

Found: Potbellied Pig

Two phone numbers followed: one to call during the day and another to call at night. I'd never seen such an announcement. Similar ones, sure.

Found: Black Retriever
Found: Psychedelic Skateboard
Found: Gold Brooch

But "Found: Potbellied Pig"? Who loses a pig? Who *owns* a pig? I know many pet owners, but pet-pig owners? Can you imagine providing daily care for a pig? (Denalyn says she can.) Do pig owners invite dinner guests to pet the pig? Do they hang a sign on the outside gate: "Potbelly on Patrol"? Pig owners must be a special breed.

Even more so, those who rescue them. The sign presupposes a curious moment. Someone spotted the pig lumbering down the sidewalk. "Poor thing. Climb in little piggy, piggy, piggy. The street is no place for a lonely sow. I'll take you home."

Suppose one appeared on your porch. Upon hearing a snort at your front door, would you open it? Not me. Golden retriever? You bet. German shepherd? Will do. St. Bernard? Count on me for a few nights and a few neighborhood signs. But a potbellied pig? Sorry. I'd leave him on Jericho Road.

I wouldn't claim one. But God would. God did. God did when he claimed us.

We assume God cares for the purebreds of the world. The clean-nosed, tidy-living, convent-created souls of society. When God sees French poodles and Great Danes wandering the streets, he swings his door open. But what about the rest of us? We're prone to wander too. We find ourselves far from home. Do we warrant his oversight?

Psalm 91 offers a rousing yes! If you need to know the nature and size of God's lordship, nestle under the broad branches of David's poetry.

> Those who live in the shelter of the Most High
>
> > will find rest in the shadow of the Almighty.
>
> This I declare of the LORD:

He alone is my refuge, my place of safety;

he is my God, and I am trusting him.

For he will rescue you from every trap

and protect you from the fatal plague.

He will shield you with his wings.

He will shelter you with his feathers.

His faithful promises are your armor and protection.

Do not be afraid of the terrors of the night,

nor fear the dangers of the day,

nor dread the plague that stalks in darkness,

nor the disaster that strikes at midday.

Though a thousand fall at your side,

though ten thousand are dying around you,

these evils will not touch you.

But you will see it with your eyes;

you will see how the wicked are punished.

If you make the LORD your refuge,

if you make the Most High your shelter,

no evil will conquer you;

no plague will come near your dwelling.

For he orders his angels

to protect you wherever you go.

They will hold you with their hands

to keep you from striking your foot on a stone.

You will trample down lions and poisonous snakes;

you will crush fierce lions and serpents under your feet!

The LORD says, "I will rescue those who love me.

I will protect those who trust in my name.

When they call on me, I will answer;

I will be with them in trouble.

I will rescue them and honor them.

I will satisfy them with a long life

and give them my salvation."

(Ps. 91:1–16)

Sixteen verses collaborate to envision one image: God as your guardian. See if you can spot the most common word of the psalm:

"Those who live in the shelter of the Most High *will* find rest."

"He *will* rescue you."

"He *will* shield you."

"He *will* shelter you."

"Evils *will* not touch you."

"They [angels] *will* hold you."

"The LORD says, 'I *will* rescue.'"

"I *will* protect."

"I *will* answer."

"I *will* be with them."

"I *will* rescue."

"I *will* satisfy."

Okay, I gave you a good hint, but I don't want you to miss this point: God offers more than the possibility of protection or the likelihood of protection. Will God guard you? Is the pope Catholic? Your serenity matters to heaven. God's presence encapsulates your life. Separating you from evil is God, your guardian.

During the Clinton-Lewinsky scandal, special prosecutor Kenneth Starr spoke at our church. Because of the combustible days, a couple of tougher-than-two-dollar-steak U.S. marshals monitored his every move. One walked ahead, the other behind. Between services they silently sized up all well-wishers. While Judge Starr sat in the break room, they stood at the door, the American version of Great Britain's Foot Guards. When I asked if he minded their presence, Judge Starr shrugged. "You know, their protection comforts."

So much more does God's. He sizes up every person who comes your way. As you walk, he leads. As you sleep, he patrols. "He will shield you with his wings. He will shelter you with his feathers" (v. 4).

The image of living beneath *Shaddai*'s shadow reminds me of a rained-out picnic. My college friends and I barely escaped a West Texas storm before it pummeled the park where we were spending a Saturday afternoon. As we were leaving, my buddy brought the car to a sudden stop and gestured to a tender sight on the ground. A mother bird sat exposed to the rain, her wing extended over her baby who had fallen out of the nest. The fierce storm prohibited her from returning to the tree, so she covered her child until the wind passed.

From how many winds is God protecting you? His wing, at this moment, shields you. A slanderous critic heading toward your desk is interrupted by a phone call. A burglar en route to your house has a flat tire. A drunk driver runs out of gas before your car passes his. God, your guardian, protects you from

"every trap" (v. 3);
"the fatal plague" (v. 3);
"the plague that stalks in darkness" (v. 6);
"the terrors of the night . . . the dangers of the day" (v. 5).

One translation boldly promises: "Nothing bad will happen to you" (v. 10 NCV).

"Then why does it?" someone erupts. "Explain my job transfer. Or the bum who called himself my dad. Or the death of our child." Here is where potbellied-pig thoughts surface. God protects Alaskan malamutes and English setters, but little runts like me? Perhaps your Rubik's Cube has a square that won't turn. If God is our guardian, why do bad things happen to us?

Have they? Have bad things *really* happened to you? You and God may have different definitions for the word *bad*. Parents and children do. Look up the word *bad* in a middle-schooler's dictionary, and you'll read definitions such as "pimple on nose," "Friday night all alone," or "pop quiz in geometry." "Dad, this is really bad!" the youngster says. Dad, having been around the block a time or two, thinks differently. Pimples pass. And it won't be long before you'll treasure a quiet evening at home. Inconvenience? Yes. Misfortune? Sure. But *bad?* Save that adjective for emergency rooms and cemeteries.

What's bad to a child isn't always bad to a dad.

What you and I might rate as an absolute disaster, God may rate as a pimple-level problem that will pass. He views your life the way you view a movie after you've read the book. When something bad happens, you feel the air sucked out of the theater. Everyone else gasps at the crisis on the screen. Not you. Why? You've read the book. You know how the good guy gets out of the tight spot. God views your life with the same confidence. He's not only read your story . . . he wrote it. His perspective is different, and his purpose is clear.

God uses struggles to toughen our spiritual skin.

Consider it a sheer gift, friends, when tests and challenges come at you from all sides. You know that under pressure, your faith-life is forced into the open and shows its true colors. So don't try to get out of anything prematurely. Let it do its work so you become mature and well-developed, not deficient in any way. (James 1:2–4 MSG)

One of God's cures for weak faith? A good, healthy struggle. Several years ago our family visited Colonial Williamsburg, a re-creation of eighteenth-century America in Williamsburg, Virginia. If you ever visit there, pay special attention to the work of the silversmith. The craftsman places an ingot of silver on an anvil and pounds it with a sledgehammer. Once the metal is flat enough for shaping, into the furnace it goes. The worker alternately heats and pounds the metal until it takes the shape of a tool he can use.

Heating, pounding.

Heating, pounding.

Deadlines, traffic.

Arguments, disrespect.

Loud sirens, silent phones.

Heating, pounding.

Heating, pounding.

Did you know that the *smith* in *silversmith* comes from the old English word *smite*? Silversmiths are accomplished smiters. So is God. Once the worker is satisfied with the form of his tool, he begins to planish and pumice it. Using smaller hammers and abrasive pads, he taps, rubs, and decorates. And no one stops him. No one yanks the hammer out of his hand and says, "Go easy on that silver. You've pounded enough!" No, the craftsman buffets the metal until he is finished with it. Some silversmiths, I'm told, keep polishing until they can see their face in the tool. When will God stop with you? When he sees his reflection in you. "The LORD will *perfect* that which concerns me" (Ps. 138:8 NKJV, emphasis mine). Jesus said, "My Father never stops working" (John 5:17).

God guards those who turn to him. The pounding you feel does not suggest his distance, but proves his nearness. Trust his sovereignty. Hasn't he earned your trust?

Has he ever spoken a word that proved to be false? Given a promise that proved to be a lie? Decades of following God led Joshua to conclude: "Not a word failed of any good thing which the LORD had spoken" (Josh. 21:45 NKJV). Look up *reliability* in heaven's dictionary and read its one-word definition: God. "If we are faithless he always remains faithful. He cannot deny his own nature" (2 Tim. 2:13 PHILLIPS).

Make a list of his mistakes. Pretty short, eh? Now make a list of the times he has forgiven you for yours. Who on earth has such a record? "The One who called you is completely dependable. If he said it, he'll do it!" (1 Thess. 5:24 MSG).

You can depend on him. He is "the same yesterday and today and forever" (Heb. 13:8 ESV). And because he is the Lord, "He will be the stability of your times" (Isa. 33:6 NASB).

Trust him. "But when I am afraid, I put my trust in you" (Ps. 56:3). Join with Isaiah, who resolved, "I will trust in him and not be afraid" (Isa. 12:2).

God is directing your steps and delighting in every detail of your life (Ps. 37:23–24). Doesn't matter who you are. Potbellied pig or prized purebred? God sees no difference. But he does see you. In fact, that's his car pulling over to the side of the road. That's God opening the door. And that's you climbing into the passenger seat.

There now, don't you feel safer knowing he is in control?

Part Four

Receive His
Love

FOURTEEN

Going Deep

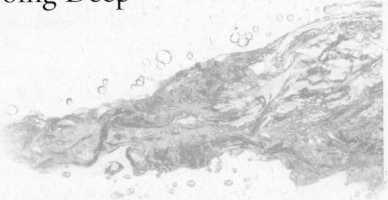

Pipín Ferreras wants to go deep, deeper than any person has ever gone. You and I are content with 10 or 20 feet of water. Certain risktakers descend 40, maybe 50. Not Pipín. This legendary Cuban diver has descended into 531 feet of ocean water, armed with nothing but flippers, a wet suit, deep resolve, and one breath of air.

His round trip lasted three minutes and twelve seconds. To prepare for such a dive, he loads his lungs with 8.2 liters of air—nearly twice the capacity of a normal human being—inhaling and exhaling for several minutes, his windpipe sounding like a bicycle pump. He then wraps his knees around the crossbar of an aluminum sled that lowers him to the sea bottom.[1]

No free diver has gone farther. Still, he wants more. Though he's acquainted with water pressure that tested World War II submarines, it's not enough. The mystery of the deep calls him. He wants to go deeper.

Could I interest you in a similar ear-popping descent? Not into the waters of the ocean, but into the limitless love of God.

> May your roots go down deep into the soil of God's marvelous love. And may you have the power to understand, as all God's people should, how wide, how long, how high, and how deep his love really is. May you experience the love of Christ, though it is so great you will never fully understand it. Then you will be filled with the fullness of life and power that comes from God. (Eph. 3:17–19)

When Paul wants to describe the love of God, he can't avoid the word *deep*. Dig "deep into the soil of God's marvelous love" (v. 17). Discover "how deep his love really is" (v. 18).

Envision Ferreras deep beneath the ocean surface. Having plunged the equivalent of five stories, where can he turn and not see water? To the right, to the left, beneath him, above him—the common consistency of his world is water. Water defines his dives, dictates his direction, liberates him, limits him. His world is water.

Can a person go equally deep into God's love? Sink so deep that he or she sees nothing but? David Brainerd, the eighteenth-century missionary to American Indians, would say so. He journaled:

> I withdrew to my usual place of retirement, in great tranquility. I knew only to breathe out my desire for a perfect conformity to Him in all things. God was so precious that the world with all its enjoyments seemed infinitely vile. I had no more desire for the favor of men than for pebbles.
>
> At noon I had the most ardent longings after God which I ever felt in my life.

In my secret retirement, I could do nothing but tell my dear Lord in a sweet calmness that He knew I desired nothing but Him, nothing but holiness, that He had given me these desires and He only could give the thing desired.

I never seemed to be so unhinged from myself, and to be so wholly devoted to God.

My heart was swallowed up in God most of the day.[2]

For any desiring a descent into such love, Scripture offers an anchor. Grab hold of this verse and let it lower you down: "God is love" (1 John 4:16).

One word into the passage reveals the supreme surprise of God's love—it has nothing to do with you. Others love you because of you, because your dimples dip when you smile or your rhetoric charms when you flirt. Some people love you because of you. Not God. He loves you because he is he. He loves you because he decides to. Self-generated, uncaused, and spontaneous, his constant-level love depends on his choice to give it. "The LORD did not set his affection on you and choose you because you were more numerous than other peoples, for you were the fewest of all peoples. But it was because the LORD loved you" (Deut. 7:7–8 NIV).

You don't influence God's love. You can't impact the treeness of a tree, the skyness of the sky, or the rockness of a rock. Nor can you affect the love of God. If you could, John would have used more ink: "God is *occasional* love" or "*sporadic* love" or "*fair-weather* love." If your actions altered his devotion, then God would not be love; indeed, he would be human, for this is human love.

And you've had enough of human love. Haven't you? Enough guys wooing you with Elvis-impersonator sincerity. Enough tabloids telling you that true love is just a diet away. Enough helium-filled expectations of bosses and parents and pastors. Enough mornings smelling like the mistakes you made while searching for love the night before.

Don't you need a fountain of love that won't run dry? You'll find one on a stone-cropped hill outside Jerusalem's walls where Jesus hangs, cross-nailed and thorn-crowned. When you feel unloved, ascend this mount. Meditate long and hard on heaven's love for you. Both eyes beaten shut, shoulders as raw as ground beef, lips bloody and split. Fists of hair yanked from his beard. Gasps of air escaping his lungs. As you peer into the crimsoned face of heaven's only Son, remember this: "God showed his great love for us by sending Christ to die for us while we were still sinners" (Rom. 5:8).

Don't trust other yardsticks. We often do. The sight of the healthy or successful prompts us to conclude, *God must really love him. He's so blessed with health, money, good looks, and skill.*

Or we gravitate to the other extreme. Lonely and frail in the hospital bed, we deduce, *God does not love me. How could he? Look at me.*

Rebuff such thoughts! Success signals God's love no more than struggles indicate the lack of it. The definitive, God-sanctioned gauge is not a good day or a bad break but the dying hours of his Son. Consider them often. Let the gap between trips to the cross diminish daily. Discover what Brainerd meant when he said, "My heart was swallowed up in God most of the day." Accept this invitation of Jesus: "Abide in My love" (John 15:9 NASB).

When you abide somewhere, you live there. You grow familiar with the surroundings. You don't pull in the driveway and ask, "Where is the garage?" You don't consult the blueprint to find the kitchen. To abide is to be at home.

To abide in Christ's love is to make his love your home. Not a roadside park or hotel room you occasionally visit, but your preferred dwelling. You rest in him. Eat in him. When thunder claps, you step beneath his roof. His walls secure you from the winds. His fireplace warms you from the winters of life. As John urged, "We take up permanent residence in a life of love" (1 John 4:16 MSG). You abandon the old house of false love and move into his home of real love.

Adapting to this new home takes time. First few nights in a new home you can wake up and walk into a wall. I did. Not in a new home, but in a motel. Climbed out of bed to get a glass of water, turned left, and flattened my nose. The dimensions to the room were different.

The dimensions of God's love are different too. You've lived a life in a house of imperfect love. You think God is going to cut you as the coach did, or abandon you as your father did, or judge you as false religion did, or curse you as your friend did. He won't, but it takes time to be convinced.

For that reason, abide in him. Hang on to Christ the same way a branch clutches the vine. According to Jesus, the branch models his definition of *abiding*. "As the branch cannot bear fruit of itself unless it abides in the vine, so neither can you unless you abide in Me" (John 15:4 NASB).

Does a branch ever release the vine? Only at the risk of death. Does the branch ever stop eating? Nope. It receives nutrients twenty-four hours a day. Would you say the branch is vine-dependent? I would. If branches had seminars, the topic would be "Get a Grip: Secrets of Vine Grabbing." But branches don't have seminars because attendance requires releasing the vine, something they refuse to do.

How well do you pass the vine test? Do you ever release yourself from Christ's love? Go unnourished? Do you ever stop drinking from his reservoir? Do so at the certain risk of a parched heart. Do so and expect a roundworm existence.

By sealing itself off against the world, the roundworm can endure extended seasons of drought. It essentially shuts down all systems. Releasing water until it's as dry as a cotton ball, the roundworm enters a state known as anhydrobiosis, meaning "life without water." A quarter of its body weight is converted to a material that encircles and protects its inner organs. It then shrinks to about 7 percent of its normal size and waits out the dry spell.[3]

Scientists assure us that humans can't do this. I'm not so sure.

- My friend's wife left him. "Now that the kids are grown," she announced, "it's my time to have fun."

- Recent headlines told of a man who murdered his estranged wife and kids. His justification? If he can't have them, no one will.

- Yesterday's e-mail came from a good man with a persistent porn problem. He's not convinced that God can forgive him.

Anhydrobiosis of the heart. In-drawn emotions. Callous souls. Coiled and re-coiled against the love drought of life. Hard shelled to survive the harsh desert. We were not made to live this way. What can we do?

From the file entitled "It Ain't Gonna Happen," I pull and pose this suggestion. Let's make Christ's command a federal law.

Everyone has to make God's love his or her home. Let it herewith be stated and hereby declared:

> *No person may walk out into the world to begin the day*
> *until he or she has stood beneath the cross to receive God's love.*

Cabbies. Presidents. Preachers. Tooth pullers and truck drivers. All required to linger at the fountain of his favor until all thirst is gone. I mean a can't-drink-another-drop satisfaction. All hearts hydrous. Then, and only then, are they permitted to enter the interstates, biology labs, classrooms, and boardrooms of the world.

Don't you ache for the change we'd see? Less honking and locking horns, more hugging and helping kids. We'd pass fewer judgments and more compliments. Forgiveness would skyrocket. How could you refuse to give a second chance when God has made your life one big mulligan? Doctors would replace sedative prescriptions with Scripture meditation: "Six times an hour reflect on God's promise: *'I have loved you with an everlasting love'*" (Jer. 31:3 NASB, emphasis mine). And can't you hear the newscast? "Since the implementation of the love law, divorce rates have dropped, cases of runaway children have plummeted, and Republicans and Democrats have disbanded their parties and decided to work together."

Wild idea? I agree. God's love can't be legislated, but it can be chosen. Choose it, won't you? For the sake of your heart. For the sake of your home. For Christ's sake, and yours, choose it. The prayer is as powerful as it is simple: "Lord, I receive your love. Nothing can separate me from your love."

My friend Keith took his wife, Sarah, to Cozumel, Mexico, to celebrate their anniversary. Sarah loves to snorkel. Give her fins, a mask, and a breathing tube, and watch her go deep. Down she swims, searching for the mysteries below.

Keith's idea of snorkeling includes fins, a mask, and a breathing tube, but it also includes a bellyboard. The surface satisfies him.

Sarah, however, convinced him to take the plunge. Forty feet offshore, she shouted for him to paddle out. He did. The two plunged into the water where she showed him a twenty-foot-tall submerged cross. "If I'd had another breath," he confessed, "the sight would have taken it away."

Jesus waves for you to descend and see the same. Forget surface glances. No more sunburned back. Go deep. Take a breath and descend so deeply into his love that you see nothing else.

Join the psalmist in saying:

> Whom have I in heaven but you?
>> And earth has nothing I desire besides you.
> My flesh and my heart may fail,
>> but God is the strength of my heart
>> and my portion forever. . . .
> My heart has heard you say, "Come and talk
>> with me, O my people." And my heart responds,
>> "Lord, I am coming."
> (Ps. 73:25–26 NIV; 27:8 TLB)

FIFTEEN

Have You Heard the Clanging Door?

Nine-year-old Al trudges through the London streets, his hand squeezing a note, his heart pounding with fear. He has not read the letter; his father forbade him to do so. He doesn't know the message, but he knows its destination. The police station.

Young boys might covet a trip to the police station. Not Al. At least not today. Punishment, not pleasure, spawned this visit. Al failed to meet the family curfew. The fun of the day made him forget the time of day, so he came home late and in trouble.

His father, a stern disciplinarian, met Al at the front door and, with no greeting, gave him the note and the instruction, "Take it to the jailhouse." Al has no idea what to expect, but he fears the worst.

The fears prove justifiable. The officer, a friend of his father, opens the note, reads it, and nods. "Follow me." He leads the wide-eyed youngster to a jail cell, opens the door, and tells him to enter. The officer clangs the door shut. "This is what we do to naughty boys," he explains and walks away.

Al's face pales as he draws the only possible conclusion. He has crossed his father's line. Exhausted his supply of grace. Outspent the cache of mercy. So his dad has locked him away. Young Al has no reason to think he'll ever see his family again.

He was wrong. The jail sentence lasted only five minutes. But those five minutes felt like five months. Al never forgot that day. The sound of the clanging door, he often told people, stayed with him the rest of his life.[1]

Easy to understand why. Can you imagine a more ominous noise? Its echo wordlessly announced, "Your father rejects you. Search all you want; he isn't near. Plead all you want; he won't hear. You are separated from your father's love."

The slamming of the cell door. Many fear they have heard it. Al forgot the curfew. You forgot your virtue. Little Al came home late. Maybe you came home drunk. Or didn't come home at all. Al lost track of time. You lost your sense of direction and ended up in the wrong place doing the wrong thing, and heaven knows, heaven has no place for the likes of . . . Cheaters. Aborters. Adulterers. Secret sinners. Public scoundrels. Impostors. Church hypocrites. Locked away, not by an earthly father, but by your heavenly one. Incarcerated, not in a British jail, but in personal guilt, shame. No need to request mercy; the account is empty. Make no appeal for grace; the check will bounce. You've gone too far.

The fear of losing a father's love exacts a high toll. Al spent the rest of his life hearing the clanging door. That early taste of terror contributed to his lifelong devotion to creating the same in others. For Al—Alfred Hitchcock—made a career out of scaring people.

You may be scaring some folks yourself. You don't mean to. But you cannot produce what you do not possess. If you aren't convinced of God's love, how can you love others?

Do you fear you have heard the clanging door? If so, be assured. You have not. Your imagination says you did; logic says you did; some parent or pulpiteer says you did. But according to the Bible, according to Paul, you did not.

> And I am convinced that nothing can ever separate us from his love. Death can't, and life can't. The angels can't, and the demons can't. Our fears for today, our worries about tomorrow, and even the powers of hell can't keep God's love away. Whether we are high above the sky or in the deepest ocean, nothing in all creation will ever be able to separate us from the love of God that is revealed in Christ Jesus our Lord. (Rom. 8:38–39)

The words are the "Eureka!" at the end of Paul's love hunt. He initiates his search with five life-changing questions.

Question one: "If God is for us, who can ever be against us?" (v. 31). The presence of God tilts the scales of security forever in our direction. Who could hurt us?

Question two: "Since God did not spare even his own Son but gave him up for us all, won't God, who gave us Christ, also give us everything else?" (v. 32). Would God save our soul and then leave us to fend for ourselves? Will he address eternal needs and ignore earthly? Of course not.

Question three poses: "Who dares accuse us whom God has chosen for his own? Will God? No! He is the one who has given us right standing with himself" (v. 33). Once God accepts you, what other opinion matters? Every voice that accuses you, including your own, sounds wimpy in the tribunal of heaven. God's acceptance trumps earthly rejection.

Question four continues: "Who then will condemn us? Will Christ Jesus? No, for he is the one who died for us and was raised to life for us and is sitting at the place of highest honor next to God, pleading for us" (v. 34). Adjacent to God, within whispering distance of your Maker, sits the One who died for you. He occupies the place of high authority. So let your accusers or your conscience speak against you. Your divine defense attorney mutes their voices. Why? Because he loves you.

Question five asks the question of this chapter, even the question of life: "Can anything ever separate us from Christ's love?" (v. 35). This question crests the top step of a great staircase. As we stand with Paul at the top, he bids us to look around for anything that can separate us from God's love. Can you name one element of life that signals the end of God's devotion?

Or as the apostle asks, "Does it mean he no longer loves us if we have trouble or calamity, or are persecuted, or are hungry or cold or in danger or threatened with death?" (v. 35). Assembling adversaries like a jailhouse lineup, Paul waves them off one by one: "not trouble, not hard times, not hatred, not hunger, not homelessness, not bullying threats, not backstabbing, not even the worst sins listed in Scripture" (v. 35 MSG). No one can drive a wedge between you and God's love. "No, despite all these things, overwhelming victory is ours through Christ, who loved us" (v. 37). Earthly affliction does not equate to heavenly rejection.

Paul is convinced of this! He turns to the musician who holds the cymbals and gives him the nod. "And I am convinced that nothing can ever separate us from his love" (v. 38). He uses the perfect tense, implying, "I have become and I remain convinced." This is no passing idea or fluffy thought but rather a

deeply rooted conviction. Paul is convinced. What do you suppose convinced him?

Maybe the disciples did. Paul gives no clue, so I'm just specu-
lating, but maybe he asked the followers of Jesus to describe the
length of God's love. In quick response they talked of the Passover
party. It promised to be a great night. Good food. Good friends.
Uninterrupted time with Christ. But in the middle of the meal,
Jesus had dropped a bombshell: "Tonight all of you will desert me"
(Matt. 26:31).

The disciples scoffed at the idea. "Peter declared, 'Even if everyone else deserts you, I never will.' . . . And all the other disciples
vowed the same" (vv. 33, 35). "Abandon Jesus? Impossible. He's
the flypaper; we're the flies." "In his corner, in his pocket. You can
count on us, right?"

Wrong. Before the dark became dawn "all his disciples
deserted him and ran away" (Mark 14:50). John. Andrew. They
ran. Bartholomew. James. Thaddaeus. They scooted. When the
Romans appeared, the followers disappeared in a blur of knees
and elbows. Those mighty men who are today stained-glassed in
a thousand cathedrals spent the night crawling beneath donkeys
and hiding in haystacks. They abandoned him and ran away.
When the kitchen got hot, they got out. Amazing.

But even more amazing is this. When Christ rose from the
dead, he never brought it up. Never. Not even one "I told you so."
Entering the Upper Room of vow violators, he could have quoted
to them their own words, reminded them of their betrayal. "Boy,
Andrew, some friend you are. And, John, to think I was going to
let you write one of the Gospels."

He could have left them hearing the sound of a closing door.
But he didn't. "That evening, on the first day of the week, the

137

disciples were meeting behind locked doors because they were afraid of the Jewish leaders. Suddenly, Jesus was standing there among them! 'Peace be with you,' he said" (John 20:19).

They outran the guards. But they couldn't outrun the love of Christ.

Did Paul hear this story? If so, it would have been enough to convince him. Desert Jesus, and he'll still love you.

Peter might strengthen the verb. He might upgrade *desert* to *deny. Deny Jesus, and he'll still love you.* For while Christ faced a trial, Peter faced his own. As he warmed near a fire, "a servant girl came over and said to him, 'You were one of those with Jesus the Galilean.' But Peter denied it in front of everyone. 'I don't know what you are talking about,' he said" (Matt. 26:69–70).

Oh, the bouncing faith of Peter. It soared so high, Christ nick-named him the Rock (Matt. 16:16–19); plummeted so low, Jesus called him Satan (Matt. 16:21–23). Who promised loyalty more insistently? Who fell more inexcusably?

Others we might understand, but this is Peter denying Jesus. His feet walked on water. His hands distributed the miracle food to the five thousand. His eyes saw Moses and Elijah stand-ing next to Jesus on Transfiguration Hill. His lips swore alle-giance. Remember what Jesus told him? "'Before the rooster crows, you will deny me three times.' 'No!' Peter insisted. 'Not even if I have to die with you! I will never deny you!'" (Matt. 26:34–35).

But he did. Thrice. Salting the air with vulgarity, he cursed the name of his dearest friend. Then the rooster crowed. Don't you know the crowing of the bird had the effect of a cell-door clang? "At that moment the Lord turned and looked at Peter. Then Peter remembered that the Lord had said, 'Before the rooster crows tomorrow morning, you will deny me three times.' And Peter left the courtyard, crying bitterly" (Luke 22:61–62).

Jesus will never look at me again, Peter must have thought.

He was wrong. Days after the resurrection Peter and some other disciples decided to go back to Galilee and fish. Why? Why would a witness of the resurrection go fishing? He may have been hungry. Or he may have been unconvinced. Christ can defeat death, but can he love a two-timer? Maybe Peter had his doubts.

If so, the doubts began to fade when he heard the voice. Jesus called to his friends, urging them to cast their net on the right side of the boat. The fact that they didn't recognize Jesus didn't keep them from trying. After they pulled in a large haul of fish, John recognized the Master. "It is the Lord!" (John 21:7 NKJV). Peter barely got his britches on before he bailed out of the boat and swam toward Christ. Before long, the two were standing, of all places, next to a fire. Peter had denied Christ at the first fire, but he couldn't deny the love of Christ at this one.

Maybe Peter told this story to Paul. Maybe by the time he finished, Paul was brushing away a tear and saying, "I'm convinced. Nothing can separate us from God's love."

"Deny Jesus," Peter testified, "and he'll still love you."

"Doubt Jesus," Thomas could add, "and the same is true."

Thomas had his doubts. Didn't matter to him that ten sets of eyes had seen the resurrected Jesus. Or that the women who had watched him being placed in the tomb watched him walk into the room. Let them shout and clap; Thomas was going to sit and wait. He wasn't in the room when Jesus came in. Maybe he was out for bagels, or maybe he took the death of Jesus harder than the others. In one of the four times he is quoted in Scripture, Thomas pledges, "Let's go, too—and die with Jesus" (John 11:16).

Thomas would die for Christ. Surely he'd die for the chance to see the risen Christ. But he wasn't about to be fooled. He'd buried his hopes once, thank you. Not about to bury them again. No matter what the others said, he needed to see for himself. So for seven days he sat. Others rejoiced; he resisted. They celebrated; he was silent. Thomas needed firsthand evidence. So Jesus gave it. First one hand, then the other, then the pierced side. "Put your finger here and see my hands. Put your hand into the wound in my side. Don't be faithless any longer. Believe!" (John 20:27).

And Thomas did. "My Lord and my God!" (v. 28).

Only a God could come back from the dead. And only a God of love would come back for a doubter.

Desert God—he'll still love you.

Deny God—he'll still love you.

Doubt God—he'll still love you.

Paul was convinced. Are you? Are you convinced that you have never lived a loveless day? Not one. Never unloved. Those times you deserted Christ? He loved you. You hid from him; he came looking for you.

And those occasions you denied Christ? Though you belonged to him, you hung with them, and when his name surfaced, you cursed like a drunken sailor. God let you hear the crowing of conscience and feel the heat of tears. But he never let you go. Your denials cannot diminish his love.

Nor can your doubts. You've had them. You may have them even now. While there is much we cannot know, may never know, can't we be sure of this? Doubts don't separate doubters from God's love.

The jail door has never closed. God's love supply is never

empty. "For his unfailing love toward those who fear him is as great as the height of the heavens above the earth" (Ps. 103:11).

The big news of the Bible is not that you love God but that God loves you; not that you can know God but that God already knows you! He tattooed your name on the palm of his hand. His thoughts of you outnumber the sand on the shore. You never leave his mind, escape his sight, flee his thoughts. He sees the worst of you and loves you still. Your sins of tomorrow and failings of the future will not surprise him; he sees them now. Every day and deed of your life has passed before his eyes and been calculated in his decision. He knows you better than you know you and has reached his verdict: he loves you still. No discovery will disillusion him; no rebellion will dissuade him. He loves you with an everlasting love.

I wrote parts of this chapter while staying at a Florida hotel. Early one morning I spent some time seated near an Olympic-size swimming pool. After reading the verses you just read, I lifted my gaze to see a bird swoop down out of the sky and park on the edge of the water. He dipped his beak in the pool, took a drink, and flew away. "Is that an image of your love?" I asked God. The gulp of the bird didn't diminish the water volume of the pool. Your sins and mine don't lower the love level of God.

The greatest discovery in the universe is the greatest love in the universe—God's love. "Nothing can ever separate us from his love" (Rom. 8:38). Think what those words mean. You may be separated from your spouse, from your folks, from your kids, from your hair, but you are not separated from the love of God. And you never will be. Ever.

Step to the well of his love and drink up. It may take some time to feel the difference. Occasional drinks won't bedew the evaporated heart. Ceaseless swallows will. Once filled up by his love, you'll never be the same.

Peter wasn't. He traded his boat for a pulpit and never looked back. The disciples weren't. The same men who fled the garden in fear traveled the world in faith. Thomas was never the same. If the legends be true, he carried the story of God's love for doubters and deserters all the way to India, where he, like his friends and Savior, died because of love.

The fear of love lost haunted young Al. But the joy of a love found changed the disciples. May you be changed. The next time you fear you hear a clanging door, remember, "Nothing can ever separate us from his love" (Rom. 8:38).

SIXTEEN

Fearlessly Facing Eternity

Dry mouth. Moist palms. Pulse pounding like a marching-band bass drum. Eyes darting over your shoulder. Heart vaulting into your throat. You know the feeling. You know the moment. You know exactly what it's like to see the flashing lights of the highway patrol in your rearview mirror.

Response #1? Prayer life spikes. "Oh, Lord." "God help me." "Jesus, have mercy on me a sinner." Policemen have stirred more prayers than a thousand pulpits.

Our requests are unanimous, predictable, and selfish. "Let there be a wreck down the highway." "See the kid driving the red truck, God? Send the officer after him." But he doesn't. Your back window fills with red and white strobes, floodlights, and flashing headlights, and as you pull to the side of the road, response #2 kicks in. Upward prayers become backward thoughts. *What did I do? How fast was I going? Whose dog did I hit?*

The highway patrol's version of Arnold Schwarzenegger fills your side mirror. Don't dare open your door. The second you do, his hand will Marshal Dillon its way to his holster, and he'll tell you to "stay in the car, please." Your best option is to return to prayer. Only God can help you now.

We dread such moments. Remember when the teacher took you outside the classroom? When your dad heard you climbing in the bedroom window past midnight? When my oldest daughter was small, I caught her in a misdemeanor. Anticipating my reaction, she told me, "My bottom tickles." We have a word for such moments. Judgment.

Payback. The evidence is in. The truth is out. And the policeman is standing at your door. No one likes the thought of judgment.

The Ephesian Christians didn't. They feared the judgment, not of the highway patrol, but of God. Knowing he sees all sin, knowing he hates all sin, knowing he must hate what he sees—not a comforting thought—they were afraid.

So John comforted them. He dipped the quill of his pen into the inkwell of God's love and wrote:

> As we live in God, our love grows more perfect. So we will not be afraid on the day of judgment, but we can face him with confidence because we are like Christ here in this world.
>
> Such love has no fear because *perfect love expels all fear*. If we are afraid, it is for fear of judgment, and this shows that his love has not been perfected in us. (1 John 4:17–18, emphasis mine)

"Perfect love expels all fear." Couldn't you use some fear expulsion? We can relate to the story of Louis Armstrong. The famous trumpeter grew up in rural Louisiana in the early 1900s. When he was a young boy, his Aunt Haddie often sent him to the creek for water. On one occasion, as he leaned over to fill his bucket, an alligator so scared the youngster that he dropped the pail and ran. His aunt told him to go back and get the water. "That alligator," she assured, "is just as scared of you as you are of it."

"If that's the case," he answered, "then that creek water ain't fit to drink."[1]

Alligators lurk in our creeks too. And when we see them, we react. We fear rejection, so we follow the crowd. We fear not fitting in, so we take the drugs. For fear of standing out, we wear what everyone else wears. For fear of blending in, we wear what no one else wears. For fear of sleeping alone, we sleep with anyone. For fear of not being loved, we search for love in all the wrong places.

But God flushes those fears. Those saturated in God's love don't sell out to win the love of others. They don't even sell out to win the love of God.

Do you think you need to? Do you think, *If I cuss less, pray more, drink less, study more . . . if I try harder, God will love me more*? Sniff and smell Satan's stench behind those words. We all need improvement, but we don't need to woo God's love. We change because we already have God's love. God's *perfect* love.

Perfect love is just that—perfect, a perfect knowledge of the past and a perfect vision of the future. You cannot shock God with your actions. There will never be a day that you cause him to gasp, "Whoa, did you see what she just did?" Never will he turn to his angels and bemoan, "Had I known Max was going to go Spam-brained on me, I wouldn't have saved his soul." God knows your entire story, from first word to final breath, and with clear assessment declares, "You are mine."

My publisher made a similar decision with this book. Before agreeing to publish it, they read it—every single word. Multiple sets of editorial eyes scoured the manuscript, moaning at my bad jokes, grading my word crafting, suggesting a tune-up here and a tone-down there. We volleyed pages back and forth, writer to editor to writer, until finally we all agreed—this is it. It's time to publish or pass. The publisher could pass, mind you. Sometimes they do. But in this case, obviously they didn't. With perfect knowledge of this imperfect product, they signed on. What you read may surprise you, but not them.

What you do may stun you, but not God. With perfect knowledge of your imperfect life, God signed on.

Years ago I met a woman who has tasted a form of such love. Brain surgery has left her without the use of a facial nerve. As a result, she faces the world with a crooked smile. After the operation she met the love of her life. Here's how she describes him: "He sees nothing strange or ugly about me and has never, even in anger, made a joke about my appearance. He has never seen me any other way. When I look in the mirror, I see deformity, but my husband sees beauty."

See what perfect love does? It drives out the fear of judgment. In fact, it purges the fear of the day of judgment. As John wrote, "So we will not be afraid on the day of judgment, but we can face him with confidence because we are like Christ here in this world" (v. 17).

On this topic, John makes no apology and pulls no punches. The day of judgment is not a phrase in a fiction novel but a day circled on heaven's calendar. Of the twenty-seven New Testament books, only the postcard-size epistles of Philemon and Third John fail to reference our divine court appearance.[2] While the details of the day are unrevealed to us and debated by us, we know this: The day is coming. On that day, earthly wealth will not matter. Physical beauty won't be factored. Fame will be forgotten. You might be positioned next to Napoleon or Julius Caesar, but you won't ask questions about Waterloo or Brutus. All eyes will be on Christ.

Those who ignored him have high cause for fear. "Then He will also say to those on His left, 'Depart from Me, accursed ones, into the eternal fire which has been prepared for the devil and his angels'" (Matt. 25:41 NASB).

But those who accepted him have none whatsoever. "We can face him with confidence because we are like Christ here in this world" (1 John 4:17). Think about that statement. God views Christians the way he views Christ: sinless and perfect. Hence, Christians can view judgment the way Christ does: with confidence and hope. Does Jesus fear the judgment? No. A sinless soul needn't. Does Jesus fear death? No. The giver of life wouldn't. Should the Christian fear judgment or death? Not at all. "Our standing in the world is identical with Christ's" (v. 17 MSG). The Son of God stands next to you doing what the son of Joe Allbright did for me.

Joe Allbright is a fair and fearless West Texas rancher, a square-jawed, rawboned man with a neck by Rawlings. In Andrews County, where I was raised, everyone knew him.

One of Joe's sons, James, and I were best friends in high school. We played football together. (More honest, he played while I guarded the team bench.) One Friday night after an out-of-town game, James invited me to stay at his house. By the time we reached his property, the hour was way past midnight, and he hadn't told his father he was bringing anyone home.

Mr. Allbright didn't know me or my vehicle, so when I stepped out of the car in front of his house, he popped on a floodlight and aimed it right at my face. Through the glare I saw this block of a man (I think he was in his underwear), and I heard his deep voice. "Who are you?" I gulped. My mind moved at the speed of cold honey. I started to say my name but didn't. *Mr. Allbright doesn't know me.* My only hope was that James would speak up. A glacier could have melted before he did so. Finally he interceded. "It's okay, Dad. That's my friend Max. He's with me." The light went off, and Mr. Allbright threw open the door. "Come on in, boys. Food is in the kitchen."

What changed? What made Mr. Allbright flip off the light? One fact. I had aligned myself with his son. My sudden safety had nothing to do with my accomplishments or offerings. I knew his son. Period.

For the same reason, you need never fear God's judgment. Not today. Not on Judgment Day. Jesus, in the light of God's glory, is speaking on your behalf. "That's my friend," he says. And when he does, the door of heaven opens.

Trust God's love. His perfect love. Don't fear he will discover your past. He already has. Don't fear disappointing him in the future. He can show you the chapter in which you will. With perfect knowledge of the past and perfect vision of the future, he loves you perfectly in spite of both.

Perfect love can handle your fear of judgment.

(And slower driving can handle your fear of policemen.)

SEVENTEEN

If God Wrote You a Letter

Christmas comes to El Sunza, El Salvador, via the shoebox. In a village where the wealthiest make fifty dollars a month and nicer homes are distinguished by tin roofs instead of plywood, the shoebox shipment highlights the year. The delivery originates in San Antonio where the children of the church in which I serve "adopt" a Salvadoran child and prepare the boxes.

Couriers grow misty eyed describing the joy of delivery day: children squeezing their brightly wrapped box, not wanting to hurry the moment. When they finally remove the paper, eyes pop saucer-wide at the toys—a Slinky, yo-yo, doll, or truck. They find toothbrushes and toothpaste, perhaps a set of underwear or socks. But the gift they cherish most is the letter. Tucked somewhere between toys and books, occupying little space but bringing torrential excitement, is a handwritten note.

The envelope bears the child's name. José Castillo. Beatrice Gonzales. Lines form around the translators as, one by one, the children hear words intended for their ears.

"Dear Diego," one might read. "My name is Matthew. I am in the fourth grade. Do you go to school? I play soccer. Do you? We call my dog Scratch because he itches all the time . . ."

Or,

"Dear Maria, this is Kara. I would like to meet you someday. Mom says El Salvador is 'forever' from here. What do you like to do? I love to sing and read and listen to Max Lucado preach sermons." (Some of these children show such taste.)

Many of the Salvadoran kids sleep with their notes, amazed that someone in far-off Texas is thinking about them. Astounding what a letter from afar can do for children.

But you know that. Like the gifts of the children, your gifts come from a distant land. Unlike the village children, you have Christmas every day. Your shoebox bears, not toys and books, but God himself!

His work: on the cross and in the resurrection. As a result, your sin brings no guilt, and the grave brings no fear.

His energy: it's not up to you. You can do all things through Christ, who gives you strength.

His lordship: he is in charge of you and looks out for you.

His love: what can separate you from it?

Who could imagine such gifts? Who could imagine not opening them? Curiously, some of the Salvadoran children have to be told to open theirs. Bless their hearts, they think the box is the gift. It outpaces any prior possession. Some see the bright ribbon and colorful wrapping and think, *This is it. This is the present.* Were no one to tell them, they would carry the box to their dirt-floored home, place it in a prime location, and admire it, display it, but never open it.

Don't we do the same with Christ? Aren't we prone to keep

him at arm's length? We place him on the mantel of our heart: respect him, revere his name, but never open his gifts. Never dig into the box. Never unpack his presence on the dirt floor of our worry and work, sin and sorrows.

He is so willing to enter your world. The hospital room? He goes there. Late-night deadlines? He'll stay up with you. Are you watching the slow death of someone you love? He'll sit by your side every single minute. Just invite him. "Look! Here I stand at the door and knock. If you hear me calling and open the door, I will come in, and we will share a meal as friends" (Rev. 3:20).

Don't make the mistake that the associates of Lawrence of Arabia made. He took them to Paris after World War I. They had never seen such sights. The Arc de Triomphe, Napoleon's tomb, the Champs Élysées. But nothing impressed these men from the Arabian Desert more than the faucet in the bathtub of their hotel room. They turned it on and off, on and off, amazed that with a twist of the wrist they could have all the water they wanted.

When the time came to leave Paris and return to the east, Lawrence found them in the bathroom with wrenches, trying to disconnect the spout. "We need faucets," they explained. "If we have them, we will have all the water we want."[1]

They didn't understand the role of the faucet. Spouts carry water, not produce it. Spigots are the tool, not the source. The valve might direct fluid, but generate it? No. We know this . . .

Or do we? Through what faucets has God poured his love into your life? A faithful church? A prayerful spouse? Time-tested traditions? A girlfriend in college or a grandma from childhood? God's water passes through many faucets. His gift comes in many packages. The treasure, however, is not the plumbing or the box, not the container of the gift. No, the treasure is the Giver himself.

On my list of things I wish I had learned earlier, this truth hovers near the top. Grace came my way packaged in a church. Congregations and their leaders changed me. But then the churches struggled, even divided. Mature men acted less than that. The box ripped, the faucet clogged, and my heart, for a time, sank.

Not a moment too soon, I heard the invitation of the still-running fountain. "If anyone is thirsty, let him come to me [not to my prophets or people] and drink" (John 7:37 NIV).

God describes himself as "the fountain of living water" (Jer. 2:13). Thank him for the faucets, but don't trust them to nourish you. Thank him for the boxes in which his gifts come. But don't fail to open them. And most of all, don't fail to read the letter. For buried amid the gifts of daily mercy and unquenchable commitment rests a letter, a personal letter. It might read something like this:

Dear child of mine,

Are you thirsty? Come and drink. ❖ I am one who comforts you. ❖ I bought you ❖ and complete you. ❖ I delight in you and claim you as my own, rejoicing over you as a bridegroom rejoices over his bride. ❖ I will never fail you or forsake you.[2]

ACCEPT MY WORK

I know your manifold transgressions and your mighty sins, ❖ yet my grace is sufficient for you. ❖ I have cast all your sins behind my back, ❖ trampled them under my feet, and thrown them into the depths of the ocean! ❖ Your sins have been washed away, ❖ swept away like the morning mists, scattered like the clouds. Oh, return to me, for I have paid the price to set you free.[3]

Your death is swallowed up in victory. ❖ I disarmed the evil rulers and authorities ❖ and broke the power of the devil, who had the power of death. ❖ Blessed are those who die in the Lord. ❖ Your citizenship is in heaven. ❖ Come, inherit the kingdom prepared for you ❖ where I will remove all of your sorrows, and there will be no more death or sadness or crying or pain.[4]

RELY ON MY ENERGY

You are worried and troubled about many things; ❖ trust me with all your heart. ❖ I know how to rescue godly people from their trials. ❖ My Spirit helps you in your distress. ❖ Let me strengthen you with my glorious power. ❖ I did not spare my Son but gave him up for you. Won't I give you everything else? ❖ March on, dear soul, with courage! ❖ Never give up. ❖ I will help you. I will uphold you.[5]

TRUST MY LORDSHIP

Trust in me always. I am the eternal Rock, ❖ your Shepherd, the Guardian of your soul. ❖ When you go through deep waters and great trouble, I will be with you. When you go through rivers of difficulty, you will not drown! When you walk through the fire of oppression, you will not be burned up; the flames will not consume you.[6]

So, don't worry. ❖ I never tire or sleep. I stand beside you. ❖ The angel of the LORD encamps around you. ❖ I hide you in the shelter of my presence. ❖ I will go ahead of you, ❖ directing your steps and delighting in every detail of your life. If you stumble, you will not fall, for I hold you by the hand. ❖ I will guide you along the best pathway for your life.[7]

Wars will break out near and far, but don't panic. ❖ I have over-come the world. ❖ Don't worry about anything; instead, pray about everything. ❖ I surround you with a shield of love.[8]

I will make you fruitful in the land of suffering, ❖ trading beauty for ashes, joy for mourning, praise for despair. ❖ I live with the low spirited and spirit crushed. I put new spirit in you and get you on your feet again. ❖ Weeping may go on all night, but joy comes with the morning. ❖ If I am for you, who can ever be against you?[9]

RECEIVE MY LOVE

I throw my arms around you, lavish attention on you, and guard you as the apple of my eye. ❖ I rejoice over you with great glad-ness. ❖ My thoughts of you cannot be counted; they outnumber the grains of sand! ❖ Nothing can ever separate you from my love. Death can't, and life can't. The angels can't, and the demons can't. Your fears for today, your worries about tomorrow, and even the powers of hell can't keep my love away.[10]

You sometimes say, "The Lord has deserted me; the Lord has for-gotten me." But can a mother forget her nursing child? Can she feel no love for a child she has borne? Even if that were possible, I would not forget you! ❖ I paid for you with the precious lifeblood of Christ, my sinless, spotless Lamb. ❖ No one will snatch you away from me. ❖ See, I have written your name on my hand. ❖ I call you my friend. ❖ Why, the very hairs on your head are all numbered. So don't be afraid; you are valuable to me.[11]

Give me your burdens; I will take care of you. ✤ I know how weak you are, that you are made of dust. ✤ Give all your worries and cares to me, because I care about what happens to you.[12]

Remember, I am at hand. ✤ Come to me when you are weary and carry heavy burdens, and I will give you rest. ✤ I delight in you, ✤ and I can be trusted to keep my promises. ✤ Come and drink the water of life.[13]

Your Maker, your Father,
God

READER'S GUIDE

COME THIRSTY

PREPARED BY STEVE HALLIDAY

Meagan

COME TO THE WELL

1. I know you are a better person than this. I also know it's not too late to make a change. This street you're traveling? The houses look nice, but the road goes nowhere.

   A. Are you satisfied with the life you're leading? Explain.

   B. Do you ever feel that it's too late to make a change? If so, explain.

   C. What street are you currently traveling? Where does the road appear to lead?

2. Stress signals a deeper need, a longing. We long to fit in, to make a difference. Acceptance, significance—these matter to us. So we do what it takes; we go into debt to buy the house, we stretch the credit card to buy the clothes . . . and life on the treadmill begins.

   A. Describe your current stress level.

   B. What "deeper need" or "longing" can you identify in your own heart?

   C. When do you most feel as though you're living on a treadmill?

3. We spend a lot of energy going nowhere. At the end of the day, or the end of a life, we haven't moved one step. We're stuck.

   A. On what do you spend most of your energy? Is the outcome positive?

   B. Describe a time in your life that you felt stuck. What did you do to get unstuck?

   C. If you continue on your present course, where do you think you'll be in ten years? Fifteen? Twenty? Is that where you want to be? Explain.

4. "Where is God in all this?" He repeated her question. "Nearer than you've ever dreamed."

   A. What would you tell someone who asked you, "Where is God in all this?"

   B. Does God feel near to you right now? Explain.

   C. Does your present path keep you near God? What path change should you consider to keep God close?

FILL YOUR CUP

1. Read John 4:1–42.

   A. What parallels do you see between Meagan's story and the life circumstances of the woman described in John 4?

   B. Why do you think Jesus did not immediately identify himself when he met the Samaritan woman?

   C. Why do you think Jesus called attention to the woman's unsavory sexual past (vv. 16–18)?

   D. Describe Jesus's main goal in his interaction with this woman (vv. 21–24).

E. Why do you think the woman immediately became an evangelist (vv. 28–30, 39–41)?

DRINK DEEPLY

Spend a few minutes thanking God for his amazing love for you, and ask him to open your eyes to new discoveries about him and his plans for you as you read *Come Thirsty*.

ONE

The Dehydrated Heart

COME TO THE WELL

1. Deprive your soul of spiritual water, and your soul will tell you. Dehydrated hearts send desperate messages. Snarling tempers. Waves of worry. Growling mastodons of guilt and fear.

   A. How would you describe "spiritual water" to someone else? What is it?

   B. Describe a time when you felt deprived of spiritual water. What happened?

   C. What "desperate message" does your soul most often send you when you are deprived of spiritual water? How do you generally respond to this message?

2. What H_2O can do for your body, Jesus can do for your heart. Lubricate it. Aquify it. Soften what is crusty, flush what is rusty.

   A. In your life, have you needed Jesus to "lubricate" and "aquify" your heart? Explain.

   B. Describe a specific time when you allowed Jesus to soften what was crusty or flush what was rusty.

   C. Take stock of your heart at this very moment. Do you need Jesus to do anything for it? Explain.

3. In order for Jesus to do what water does, you must let him go where water goes. Deep, deep inside. Internalize him. Ingest him. Welcome him into the inner workings of your life. Let Christ be the water of your soul.

   A. How deeply do you normally allow Christ to penetrate your life? Explain.

   B. What areas of your life seem most resistant to Christ?

   C. How can you better welcome Christ into the inner workings of your life? What specific steps can you take?

4. Religion pacifies, but never satisfies. Church activities might hide a thirst, but only Christ quenches it. Drink *him*. And drink often. . . . Regular sips satisfy thirsty throats.

   A. In what way does religion pacify? Why can it never satisfy?

   B. How can church activities hide a spiritual thirst? Have they ever done so for you? If so, explain.

   C. How does one "drink" Christ? Describe the process as you know it.

FILL YOUR CUP

1. Read John 7:14–39.

   A. What do you think so amazed the religious professionals about Jesus's teaching (v. 15)?

   B. How did Jesus explain his extraordinary teaching (v. 16)?

   C. What key to effective Bible study does Jesus describe in verse 17?

   D. What miracle did Jesus perform that upset the religious professionals (v. 23)? Why did it upset them? Why did Jesus think it should not have upset them?

E. From where did Jesus claim to have come (vv. 16, 29)? Why did this upset some in the crowd?

F. What did Jesus say in verses 33–34 that confused his opponents? Why do you think Jesus spoke in such a cloaked fashion? What do you believe he really meant?

G. How do you "come" to Jesus and "drink" (v. 37)?

H. What connection does Jesus make between believing in him and living water (v. 38)?

I. What did Jesus mean by "living water" (v. 39)? Is this living water in you? Explain.

DRINK DEEPLY

Even if it is not your regular habit, schedule at least half an hour to get alone with God. Use the time both to thank him for his desire to fill you with living water and to ask him to reveal those areas of your heart that are most "dehydrated." Ask him, "Where have I not allowed the living water of Jesus to penetrate my heart? In my relationships? In my work life? In my desire for some particular thing?" Once the Lord has clearly answered your prayer, ask for the strength and wisdom to give that area over to the healing waters of Jesus.

TWO

Sin Vaccination

COME TO THE WELL

1. Sin, for a season, quenches thirst. But so does salt water. Given time, the thirst returns, more demanding and demanding more than ever.

   A. In what way does sin temporarily quench thirst? Why is it only temporary?

   B. Have you experienced the temporary thirst-quenching power of sin? Explain.

   C. In what way do the demands of sin get more demanding?

2. Lead a godless life, and expect a godless eternity. Spend a life telling God to leave you alone, and he will.

   A. How would you describe a "godless life"? What does it look like?

   B. How would you describe a "godless eternity"? What would it look like?

   C. In what ways do we tell God to leave us alone?

3. You can select your spiritual father. You can change your family tree from that of Adam to God. And when you do, he moves in. His resistance becomes your resistance.

   A. How can someone select his or her spiritual father? Describe the process.

B. Have you changed your family tree from that of Adam to God? How can you know for sure?

C. How can you tell when you're battling sin through God's resistance and not through your own?

4. Trust the work of God *for* you. Then trust the presence of Christ *in* you. Take frequent, refreshing drinks from his well of grace. You need regular reminders that you are not fatally afflicted! Don't live as though you are.

A. What does it mean to trust the work of God *for* you?

B. What does it mean to trust the presence of Christ *in* you?

C. How do some believers live as though they are fatally afflicted with sin?

FILL YOUR CUP

1. Read Ephesians 2:1–10.

A. How does Paul paint our lives before we placed our faith in Christ (vv. 1–3)?

B. What changed our desperate situation (v. 4)?

C. What did God do for us that we couldn't do ourselves (v. 5)?

D. What is yet in store for every believer (vv. 6–7)?

E. How did we receive these amazing blessings (vv. 8–9)?

F. What is expected of us now (v. 10)?

2. Read Isaiah 53:4–6.

A. Who is the "he" in verse 4?

B. What did he do for us (vv. 4–5)?

C. What have we done to make this necessary (v. 6)?

3. Read 1 John 1:5–9.

   A. How does verse 5 portray God?

   B. What hypocrisy is revealed in verse 6?

   C. What does Jesus do for us, according to verse 7? What condition do we have to meet?

   D. How do we sometimes deceive ourselves (v. 8)?

   E. What promise are we given in verse 9?

DRINK DEEPLY

Go somewhere quiet, taking your Bible with you. First, invite God to meet with you in a special way. Then turn to Psalm 51 and silently read through it. Then pray through it, this time reading it out loud, pausing after each verse to ask God to apply David's prayer to your own heart. Continue in this way through the psalm, inviting God to cleanse your heart so you might serve him with joy.

THREE

When Grace Goes Deep

COME TO THE WELL

1. Thanks to some legalistic big brothers, Paul's readers had gone from grace receiving to law keeping. Their Christian life had taken on the joy level of an upper G.I. endoscopy. Paul was puzzled.

   A. Describe the difference between "grace receiving" and "law keeping."

   B. Why does law keeping generally deflate joy?

   C. What most puzzled Paul about the choice his friends had made? Would he be puzzled if he witnessed your life? Explain.

2. The churches suffered from . . . grace blockage. The Father might let you in the gate, but you have to earn your place at the table. God makes the down payment on your redemption, but you pay the monthly installments. Heaven gives the boat, but you have to row it if you ever want to see the other shore.

   A. In your own terms, define "grace blockage."

   B. How do we sometimes try to earn our place at God's table?

   C. Why do you think we face the continual temptation to mix grace and good works?

3. Grace defines who you are. The parent you can't please is as mistaken as the doting uncle you can't disappoint. People hold no clout. Only God does. According to him, you are his. Period.

   A. Does grace define who *you* are? Explain.

   B. In what way does grace shape how you live? How did it shape the way you acted today?

   C. Have you ever let people hold the clout that belongs only to God? If so, describe what happened.

4. God's hands . . . draw together the disjointed blotches in our life and render them an expression of his love.

   A. What disjointed blotches in your life has God rendered an expression of his love?

   B. How is God working in your life right now?

   C. How do you see God's love active in the lives of your loved ones?

FILL YOUR CUP

1. Read Galatians 1:6–9; 2:16.

   A. What event greatly surprised Paul (v. 6)? Why did it surprise him?

   B. What caused this surprising event (v. 7)?

   C. What strong statement does Paul make in verse 8? Why does he say this so strongly?

   D. What is the significance of his repeating his strong statement in verse 9?

   E. How does a person get right with God, according to 2:16?

   F. Who gets right with God through perfect behavior (2:16)?

2. Read 2 Samuel 9:1–13.

    A. Why did David show such kindness to Mephibosheth (v. 1)?

    B. Why did David tell Mephibosheth not to fear (v. 7)? Why might the man have felt afraid?

    C. How did Mephibosheth see himself (v. 8)?

    D. What privilege did Mephibosheth receive (v. 11)?

    E. Why do you think the story is summarized in verse 13? What's the point?

DRINK DEEPLY

Whenever genuine grace shows up, it makes a powerful difference in the lives of those it touches. For a slight change of pace, plan an evening to gather friends or loved ones and together watch *Les Misérables,* the film adaptation of Victor Hugo's classic work. Watch it specifically for any illustrations of grace in action. Then discuss what you saw, especially in terms of its portrayal of grace.

Also, if you'd like to learn more about the wonders of God's grace, especially regarding how it can change the way you live, consider reading a quality book on the topic, such as Philip Yancey's *What's So Amazing about Grace?* or Charles Swindoll's *The Grace Awakening.*

FOUR

When Death Becomes Birth

COME TO THE WELL

1. Many of us weep at the thought of death. Do you? Do you dread your death? And is your dread of death robbing your joy of life?

   A. Answer each of Max's questions.

   B. Why is death hard for most of us to contemplate, let alone discuss?

   C. Why do we often describe the death of a loved one as "loss"?

2. Why did Jesus let Lazarus die only to call him back? To show who runs the show. To trump the cemetery card. To display the unsquashable strength of the One who danced the Watusi on the neck of the devil, who stood face to clammy face with death and declared, "You call that a dead end? I call it an escalator."

   A. Why do you think Jesus let Lazarus die?

   B. In what way has Jesus made death an escalator?

   C. How did Jesus "trump the cemetery card"? Do you think he will do this for you? Explain.

3. Dread of death ends when you know heaven is your true home.

A. How does knowing that heaven is your true home alter your thinking about death?

B. Why do many Christians still dread death?

C. Describe your true home.

4. Give God your death. Imagine your last breath, envision your final minutes, and offer them to him. Deliberately. Regularly.

A. What do you envision when you think of your final minutes?

B. What does it mean to "give God your death"? Have you done this? Explain.

C. Why is it wise to regularly think of your own death? How can you keep this from becoming morbid?

FILL YOUR CUP

1. Read Hebrews 9:27–28.

A. What is the destiny of every man and woman (v. 27)?

B. What happens after this event (v. 27)?

C. What did Christ do the first time he came to earth (v. 28)?

D. What will Christ do the second time he comes to earth (v. 28)?

2. Read Hebrews 2:14–16.

A. Why did Jesus have to become human (v. 14)?

B. What mission did Jesus accomplish by his death (vv. 14–15)?

C. What group did Jesus intend to help by his death (v. 16)?

3. Read 1 Corinthians 15:54–58.

A. When do the events described in this passage take place?

B. What specifically takes place (v. 54)?

C. How would you answer the questions in verse 55?

D. What cause and effect is described in verse 56? What provides the power?

E. What victory is described in verse 57? Who wins this victory? Who gets to enjoy this victory?

F. What conclusion does Paul draw from the truth he has just declared (v. 58)? How should these truths affect our lives?

DRINK DEEPLY

To help you grapple with your own death, write out your own obituary. Make it as long or as short as you like, but make sure it reflects the reality of your life, not merely how you hope to be remembered. What do you think survivors would really say about you?

FIVE

With Heart Headed Home

COME TO THE WELL

1. Heaven knows no stepchildren or grandchildren. You and
    Christ share the same will. What he inherits, you inherit. You
    are headed home.

    A. What does it mean that heaven knows no stepchildren or
        grandchildren?

    B. What must first happen for Christ and you to share the
        same will?

    C. When you consider heaven your true home, what
        difference does this make in the way you live right now?

2. Let your bursitis-plagued body remind you of your eternal
    one; let acid-inducing days prompt thoughts of unending
    peace. Are you falsely accused? Acquainted with abuse?
    Mudslinging is a part of this life, but not the next. Rather than
    begrudge life's troubles, listen to them.

    A. How can you allow your current troubles to remind you of
        your eternal home?

    B. What in life tends to trouble you the most? How can you
        use even this to prompt "thoughts of unending peace"?

    C. Do you tend to begrudge life's troubles or listen to them?
        Explain.

3. The more you drink from God's well, the more you urge the clock to tick. Every bump of the second hand brings you closer to a completed adoption.

    A. In what ways do you "drink from God's well"?

    B. List the things you won't miss about earthly life.

    C. What comforts you the most about your future "completed adoption"? Explain.

4. Blessings and burdens. Both can alarm-clock us out of slumber. Gifts stir homeward longings. So do struggles. Every homeless day carries us closer to the day our Father will come.

    A. Describe some blessings that have alarm-clocked you out of slumber.

    B. Describe some burdens that have alarm-clocked you out of slumber.

    C. What pictures come to mind when you think of the day your Father will come for you?

Fill Your Cup

1. Read Romans 8:15–25.

    A. What two things are contrasted in verse 15? What is important to remember about this contrast?

    B. What (or who) reminds us of our true identity (v. 16)?

    C. What promise is made in verse 17? What advisory is given?

    D. What two things are compared in verse 18? What is the point of this comparison?

    E. What future event is described in verses 19–21?

    F. What truth is proclaimed in verse 22?

G. What present truth and future reality are proclaimed in verse 23? Why is it important to keep both things in mind?

H. What are we told to do in verse 24?

I. How are we told to do this in verse 25?

2. Read Galatians 4:4–7.

A. What event is described in verse 4?

B. What two things did Christ accomplish for us, according to verse 5?

C. What cry goes out from our hearts, according to verse 6? Who prompts this cry?

D. What promise is made in verse 7?

DRINK DEEPLY

To remind you of your inheritance in Christ, take steps to get your own will in order. As you consider your own estate and where you want it to go after your death, consciously bring to mind the amazing inheritance Christ has bestowed on you.

SIX

Hope for Tuckered Town

COME TO THE WELL

1. I used to think there were two kinds of people: the saved and unsaved. Paul corrects me by describing a third: the *saved, but unspiritual.*

    A. Describe a saved person.

    B. Describe an unsaved person.

    C. Describe a saved, but unspiritual person.

    D. Which one of the three are you? Explain.

2. The unspiritual person cranks the car and hunkers behind it. Tragically, these people act "like people of the world" (1 Cor. 3:3 NCV). In language, lifestyle, priorities, and personality, they blend in with nonbelievers. They let God save them, but not change them.

    A. Describe a few expected differences between the actions of believers and "people of the world."

    B. How does your language compare with that of nonbelievers? How about your lifestyle? Priorities? Personality?

    C. What areas of your life do you think God most wants to change?

3. The saved but unspiritual see salvation the way a farmer sees a hundred acres of untilled soil—lots of work. *Church attendance, sin resistance—have I done enough?* No wonder they're tired.

    A. Do you see the Christian life as "lots of work"? Explain.

    B. What risk is there in this view of Christianity?

    C. Be honest. Do you feel tired in your walk with Christ? Explain.

4. Annual fill-ups or monthly ingestions won't do. You aren't sampling wine at a California vineyard. You're hiking through Death Valley, and that mirage you see is not a mirage but really is the river you need. Dive in and drink.

    A. What are the most personal ways you "fill up" with the Savior?

    B. What image or metaphor most clearly conveys this idea for you? Why?

    C. How do we so often "sample" Christ rather than "drink" him?

FILL YOUR CUP

1. Read Galatians 3:1–14.

    A. What question does Paul ask in verse 2? What answer is he expecting? Why is this crucial?

    B. What question does Paul ask in verse 3? What answer is he expecting?

    C. What question does Paul ask in verse 4? What answer is he expecting?

    D. What question does Paul ask in verse 5? What answer is he expecting?

E. What example does Paul give in verses 6–9? How does this example illustrate his point?

F. What general principle is given in verse 10?

G. What general principle is given in verse 11?

H. What did Christ do for us, according to verse 13?

I. Why did Christ do this for us, according to verse 14?

2. Read Ephesians 5:18.

A. What are believers instructed not to do in this verse?

B. What are believers instead instructed to do?

C. Describe someone you know who seems to be infused with the Spirit.

Drink Deeply

Sometimes the best cure for residents of Tuckered Town is simply to rest awhile in the presence of God—no other agenda, no other activity. Turn off your cell phone, go somewhere quiet, and spend at least an hour or two in God's presence—just you and him. "Be silent, and know that I am God!" (Ps. 46:10).

SEVEN

Waiting for Power

COME TO THE WELL

1. Even after a thousand campfire conversations and a scrapbook full of jaw-dropping moments, some disciples resist. *I'm still not sure.*

   A. What do you think kept these disciples from feeling sure about Jesus?

   B. What do you think keeps us from feeling sure about Jesus?

   C. In what way(s) do you sometimes feel unsure about Jesus?

2. Doubters became prophets. Peter preached, and people came, and God opened the floodgates on the greatest movement in history. It began because the followers were willing to do one thing: wait in the right place for power.

   A. What turned doubters into prophets?

   B. Why do you think God waited to send the Spirit to the disciples? Why didn't God send him immediately after Christ ascended to heaven?

   C. Is God asking you to wait for something right now? If so, what do you think he wants to teach you?

3. Unceasing prayer may sound complicated, but it needn't be that way. . . . Think of prayers less as an activity for God and more as an awareness of God. Seek to live in uninterrupted awareness. Acknowledge his presence everywhere you go.

A. What needs to change for you to start thinking of prayer as "an awareness of God"?

B. In what new ways could you acknowledge God's presence?

C. What do you expect to happen when you acknowledge God's presence everywhere you go?

4. We can only wonder what would happen today if we, who *still* struggle, did what they did: wait on the Lord in the right place.

A. In what ways do you still struggle to have faith?

B. How is the Lord asking you to wait on him right now?

C. What has happened in the past when you have waited on the Lord in the right "place"? Describe your experience.

FILL YOUR CUP

1. Read Matthew 28:16–17.

A. What group is described in this passage? What were they doing? Why were they doing it?

B. What two things happened when members of this group saw Jesus? What do you think accounts for the difference?

2. Read Luke 24:49; Acts 1:4–5.

A. What promise was Jesus talking about in Luke 24:49? How did he instruct them to receive the benefits of this promise?

B. What command did Jesus give his followers in Acts 1:4? What is the promise he mentions?

C. What promise did Jesus make in verse 5? How does this expand on his earlier statement?

3. Read Acts 2:1–4.

   A. What group is described in verse 1? Why were they there?

   B. What sound did these individuals hear (v. 2)? What is significant about it?

   C. What sight did these individuals see (v. 3)? What is significant about it?

   D. What happened to these individuals (v. 4)? What accounted for this activity?

   E. What lesson(s) can we learn for our lives today from this passage?

DRINK DEEPLY

Do a personal study of the power of the Spirit in the life of the early church. Over a number of days or weeks, sit down with your Bible and read through the book of Acts, noting in particular the passages where the Spirit's activity is specifically mentioned. You might be surprised at the vast number of ways in which the Spirit moves in power!

EIGHT

God's Body Glove

COME TO THE WELL

1. What Jesus did in Galilee is what the Holy Spirit does in us. Jesus *dwelt among* the people, teaching, comforting, and convicting. The Holy Spirit *dwells within* us, teaching, comforting, and convicting.

   A. Does the Holy Spirit "dwell within" you? How do you know for sure?

   B. What is the Holy Spirit teaching you these days?

   C. How is the Holy Spirit comforting you these days?

   D. Of what is the Holy Spirit convicting you these days?

2. Do your actions interrupt the flow of the Spirit in your life?

   A. What does it mean to "interrupt the flow of the Spirit"?

   B. How do someone's actions interrupt the flow of the Spirit?

   C. How do you know when your actions have interrupted the flow of the Spirit in your life? What do you do about this?

3. Harbored sin interferes with Spirit circulation. Confessed sin, however, splices the cable and restores the power.

   A. Define "harbored sin." Is this ever a problem in your life? Explain.

B. What does it take for you to confess your sins to God?

C. Why is confession of sin so important in the life of a growing believer?

4. *Accept* his power. . . . *Surrender* to his plan. . . . And *keep* at it.

A. How can you accept God's power in your current circumstances?

B. What does it mean *today* for you to surrender to God's plan?

C. Why is it important to keep at this discipline?

FILL YOUR CUP

1. Read Galatians 2:19–20.

A. What does it mean to be "crucified with Christ"?

B. Can you say, as did Paul, that "I myself no longer live"?

C. What does it mean to say that "Christ lives in me"?

D. How does one live "by trusting in the Son of God"?

E. What two things does Paul remind us about Christ in his last phrase of verse 20?

2. Read Romans 8:5–11.

A. How can you tell if you're living in your own strength, according to verse 5? How can you tell if you're living in the power of God?

B. What two ways of life are described in verse 6? How do they differ in outcome?

C. How does Paul describe the mind-set of those who try to live by their own power (v. 7)?

D. What blanket statement does Paul make about those who don't rely on God's power (v. 8)?

E. What definition of a Christian does Paul give in verse 9?

F. What general principle for the Christian life does Paul give in verses 10–11?

3. Read Ephesians 4:25–32.

A. What things are we to avoid, according to this passage?

B. What things are we to pursue, according to this passage?

C. How do both of these things depend on being filled with the Holy Spirit?

DRINK DEEPLY

What does it mean to be "filled with the Spirit"? Many believers make it too complicated. Really, it's just inviting the Spirit to work in you and through you. If you're not familiar with how this works, try an experiment for one week. Get a little notebook and carry it with you. Then, throughout the week, whenever you are faced with a temptation or a difficult decision or a problem or another challenge, pray that God's Holy Spirit will guide you or strengthen you or do whatever else you need him to do—and note your request in your notebook. After the week has passed, go back through your notebook to see how the Spirit really *has* filled you and done remarkable things in your life.

NINE

It's Not Up to You

COME TO THE WELL

1. The Holy Spirit invisibly, yet indispensably, serves as a rudder for the ship of your soul, keeping you afloat and on track. This is no solo journey.

    A. How does the Holy Spirit serve as the rudder for your ship?

    B. When you feel as though you're in this battle alone, how can you remind yourself that the Spirit of God is within you and for you?

    C. Describe a specific time when the Holy Spirit kept you "afloat and on track."

2. When hell's interlopers come seeking to snatch you from God, the seal turns them away. He bought you, owns you, and protects you. God paid too high a price to leave you unguarded.

    A. In your own words, describe the "seal" of the Holy Spirit.

    B. How does it make you feel to know that God guards you through the ministry of the Holy Spirit?

    C. Describe a time when you know the Holy Spirit guarded you and kept you from serious injury.

3. The father had no intention of letting the boy fall. Your Father has no intention of letting you fall, either. You can't see him, but he is present.

    A. In what situations do you feel most likely to fall?

    B. How does your Father tend to keep you from falling?

    C. Why do you think so much of God's work remains invisible to our eyes?

4. The impoverished orphan of Russia, the distraught widow of the battlefield, the aging saint in the convalescent home—they may think they have no voice, no clout, no influence. But they have a friend—a counselor, a comforter—the blessed Spirit of God, who speaks the language of heaven in heaven.

    A. When are you most likely to think you have no voice, no clout, no influence in heaven? How do you combat this?

    B. How does it make you feel to know that the Spirit of God prays for you?

    C. What can you do to help others know they have a voice and clout in heaven?

FILL YOUR CUP

1. Read Ephesians 1:13–14; 4:30.

    A. What happens to everyone who believes in Christ (v. 13)?

    B. What is one important role of the Spirit within us (v. 14)?

    C. To what future day does verse 14 look forward?

    D. Why does Paul remind us of this day in 4:30? What are we warned against doing?

2. Read Romans 8:26–27.

    A. Why does the Spirit intercede for us in our prayers (v. 26)? How can this give us great hope?

    B. How can we be sure that these prayers will *always* be effective (v. 27)? How can this give us great hope?

DRINK DEEPLY

Make a list of all the major challenges facing you at this moment. Whether these challenges occur in your home, at work, in church, in your neighborhood, or elsewhere, write them down. What strategies have you used to meet these challenges? Have your attempts worked? Commit each one of these concerns to the Lord, reminding yourself in every case that you are not alone in this battle. Keep a journal to record (1) the dates you prayed about the challenge; (2) any change you noticed in your attitude or anxiety level; (3) how God answered your prayers.

In God We (Nearly) Trust

Come to the Well

1. Typhoons test our trust in the Captain. Does God know what he is doing? Can he get us out? Why did he allow the storm?

    A. How do "typhoons" test your trust in the Captain?

    B. When was the last time you wondered, *God, do you know what you're doing?*

    C. Describe a typhoon experience that caused you to cry out to your Captain for rescue. What did this experience do for your faith?

2. No struggle will come your way apart from God's purpose, presence, and permission. What encouragement this brings! You are never the victim of nature or the prey of fate. Chance is eliminated. You are more than a weather vane whipped about by the winds of fortune.

    A. Does it comfort you to know that no struggle comes your way apart from God's purpose, presence, and permission? Explain.

    B. How is chance or fate eliminated in the life of the believer?

    C. When bad things happen to you, how do you look for God's purpose and his presence?

3. When someone you love faces adversity, don't insensitively declare, "God is in control." A cavalier tone can eclipse the right truth. Be careful.

   A. Why is it a bad idea to declare, "God is in control," without taking into account the specifics of the situation?

   B. Describe a time when you saw someone violate this guideline. What happened?

   C. In what way can a "cavalier tone" tend to "eclipse the right truth"?

4. God's ways are always right. They may not make sense to us. They may be mysterious, inexplicable, difficult, and even painful. But they are right.

   A. How do we know that God's ways are always right?

   B. Describe a time when God's ways did not make sense to you. Has hindsight provided any insight? If so, explain.

   C. Why is it important to remember that God's ways are always right?

Fill Your Cup

1. Read Daniel 4:1–37.

   A. What did Nebuchadnezzar, the mightiest king of his era, learn about the sovereign rule of God (vv. 1–3)?

   B. What dream did the king have (vv. 4–18)? Why did this dream frighten him so badly?

   C. What interpretation of the dream did Daniel give the king (vv. 19–26)?

   D. What advice did Daniel give the king (v. 27)?

    E. What happened to the king when he ignored Daniel's advice (vv. 29–33)?

    F. How did the king's experience change his outlook (v. 34)?

    G. What conclusion did the king reach regarding the sovereign rule of God (vv. 35, 37)?

2. Read Luke 22:39–44.

    A. What request did Jesus make of his Father in verse 42?

    B. What answer did he receive?

    C. What was more important to Jesus than getting a yes response to his request?

    D. How did God show Jesus that he had heard his prayer, even though he would not grant the request (v. 43)?

    E. How do we know this was a sincere request (v. 44)?

    F. How does this episode reveal that Jesus told the truth in John 4:34; 6:38–39; and 8:29?

    G. What would have been the consequences if Jesus had not trusted God?

DRINK DEEPLY

When we speak of God's sovereignty, we sometimes express it as a cold doctrine that doesn't seem to connect much with real life. To remind yourself of how God's sovereignty often works, read the biblical book of Esther. Although God's name is not mentioned in the book, his sovereign hand is evident. In what instances do you see it? In what ways do God's actions in this book echo what he's doing in your own life?

For a very different picture of the way God's sovereignty at times expresses itself, read the fourth chapter of Daniel. How do the lessons of this book differ from those of Esther?

ELEVEN

Worry? You Don't Have To

COME TO THE WELL

1. Worry changes nothing. You don't add one day to your life or one bit of life to your day by worrying. Your anxiety earns you heartburn, nothing more.

   A. What kind of things do you tend to worry about?

   B. In a given week, how often would you say you worry about something?

   C. Describe what worry has accomplished for you.

2. Worry betrays a fragile faith, an "unconscious blasphemy." We don't intentionally doubt God, but don't we, when we worry, essentially doubt God?

   A. How does worry betray a "fragile faith"? In what way is it an "unconscious blasphemy"?

   B. What's the problem with doubting God?

   C. Select one of the worries you identified in 1.A. If you aren't trusting God to take care of it, whom or what are you trusting to take care of it? What steps can you take to turn it over to God?

3. Worry diminishes as we look upward. God knows what can happen on this journey, and he wants to bring us home.

A. Why does worry diminish as we look upward?

B. How does knowing that God wants to bring us home help diminish worry?

C. How do you personally battle worry?

4. God's proof is God's past. Forgetfulness sires fearfulness, but a good memory makes for a good heart.

A. How does thinking about what God has done in the past help you in the present?

B. What good things has God done for you in the past week? The past month? The past year?

C. What most makes you afraid? How can "God's past" help you to overcome this fear?

FILL YOUR CUP

1. Read Philippians 4:6–8.

A. What are we told *not* to do in verse 6?

B. What are we told to do instead?

C. Concerning what particular things are we to do this?

D. In what particular way are we to do this?

E. What is the promised result of doing this (v. 7)?

2. Read Matthew 6:24–32.

A. According to verse 24, who is to be our "master"?

B. How does compliance with verse 24 make possible our obedience to the command of verse 25?

C. How is the illustration in verse 26 supposed to bolster our faith?

D. How would you answer the question of verse 27?

E. How would you answer the question of verse 28?

F. How is the illustration in verses 28–29 supposed to bolster our faith?

G. How would you answer the question of verse 30?

H. How is the comment in verse 32 supposed to motivate us?

3. Read 1 Peter 5:7.

A. What does this verse command?

B. To whom is this command directed?

C. What reason for the command is given?

DRINK DEEPLY

If you struggle to control your worry and anxiety, it might help to get assistance from others who have dealt with the same problem. Seek out the counsel of someone whose wisdom you respect.

Then remind yourself of a saying attributed to A. J. Cronin: "Worry never robs tomorrow of its sorrow; it only saps today of its strength." It has been said that more than 90 percent of what we worry about never happens. Test this statement in your own life. Keep a "worry journal" for three months. Divide each page into two columns: "What I Worry About" and "The Date This Worry Actually Took Shape." How many of the things you worried about in those three months actually occurred?

TWELVE

Angels Watching over You

COME TO THE WELL

1. If you believe in God's Word, you have to believe in angels. At the same time, you have to be puzzled by them.

    A. What do you believe about angels?

    B. Why does the Bible's description of angels tend to puzzle us?

    C. What is the biggest misconception about angels, in your opinion?

2. Two adjectives capture the greater truth about angels: *many* and *mighty.*

    A. What difference does it make to you that there are *many* angels?

    B. Why do you think the Bible makes a point to tell us that angels are *mighty*?

    C. Describe your favorite angel story in the Bible. Why is it your favorite?

3. Only one sound matters to angels—God's voice. Only one sight enthralls angels—God's face. They know that he is Lord of all.

    A. Do you consider it a good thing that angels respond only to God's command? Explain.

    B. What does it mean to you that God is Lord of all?

4. Refuse God at the risk of an unguarded back. But receive his lordship, and be assured that many mighty angels will guard you in all your ways.

   A. In what ways do we "refuse God"?

   B. What does it mean to "receive" God's lordship?

   C. Do you believe that angels are guarding you right now? Explain.

FILL YOUR CUP

1. Read Hebrews 1:6–7, 14; 2:2, 7, 9; 12:22; 13:2.

   A. What did God command the angels to do when Christ was born (1:6; see also Luke 2:8–15)?

   B. Name one primary angelic function (1:7).

   C. Whom are angels charged to serve (1:14)?

   D. Where do angels rank among God's creatures (2:7, 9)?

   E. Name another angelic function (12:22).

   F. Do we always know when an angel has visited us (13:2)?

2. Read Psalms 34:7; 35:1–6; 78:49; 103:20.

   A. What promise is given in Psalm 34:7?

   B. What angelic function is described in Psalm 35:5–6?

   C. What angelic function is described in Psalm 78:49?

   D. What angelic functions are described in Psalm 103:20?

DRINK DEEPLY

If you'd like to get a fuller biblical picture of the nature and activity of angels, get a good concordance and look up the words *angel* and *angels*. Then make a study of all the references you find. But be prepared for a lot of work, since Scripture uses these terms alone more than three hundred times! You might also benefit from reading what others have written about God's angelic servants: Billy Graham's *Angels* and Herbert Lockyer's *All the Angels in the Bible* are both considered classics.

THIRTEEN

With God as Your Guardian

COME TO THE WELL

1. God sizes up every person who comes your way. As you walk, he leads. As you sleep, he patrols.

    A. Do you see God as your Guardian? Explain.

    B. In what ways has God led you?

    C. Describe a time that God "patrolled" as you slept.

2. What's bad to a child isn't always bad to a dad. What you and I might rate as an absolute disaster, God may rate as a pimple-level problem that will pass.

    A. Name some things that seem bad to a child, but not to a dad.

    B. Describe a time in your life when you experienced an "absolute disaster." Did you see God's hand in this situation? Explain.

    C. How has God personally shown you his faithfulness?

3. God uses struggles to toughen our spiritual skin.

    A. How can struggles toughen our spiritual skin?

    B. How has God used struggles to toughen your spiritual skin?

    C. In what ways does it help to remember that God uses struggles to toughen our spiritual skin?

4. God guards those who turn to him. The pounding you feel does not suggest his distance, but proves his nearness. Trust his sovereignty. Hasn't he earned your trust?

   A. What does it mean to turn to God? Is this a one-time event? Explain.

   B. What "pounding" do you feel right now? How can this suggest God's nearness rather than his distance?

   C. What does it mean to trust God's sovereignty? How can you learn to do this more and more?

Fill Your Cup

1. Read Psalm 91:1–16.

   A. How does the psalmist picture God in verses 1–2? What images does he use?

   B. What additional images are used in verses 3–8? How is each image calculated to increase our trust in God?

   C. What promise is made in verses 11–12? How did the devil misuse this promise (see Matt. 4:5–7)? What can we learn from this encounter between Jesus and Satan about claiming promises?

   D. What reason does the Lord give for his actions in verse 14?

   E. What promises does God give in verses 15–16? How does an eternal perspective on life help us understand God's promises?

2. Read James 1:2–4.

   A. What does James tell us to do when troubles come our way (v. 2)?

   B. What reason does James give for his instruction (v. 3)?

C. What is the outcome of complying with James's instruction (v. 4)?

DRINK DEEPLY

Take a look at your life, especially the past ten years, and ask yourself, "What things that I once considered bad do I now consider good? How has God used the 'bad' events of my life for my good?" After you complete your personal historical survey, make sure you thank God for his good care of you—even when you don't feel it's quite what you'd have it to be.

FOURTEEN

Going Deep

COME TO THE WELL

1. Some people love you because of you. Not God. He loves you because he is he. He loves you because he decides to. Self-generated, uncaused, and spontaneous, his constant-level love depends on his choice to give it.

   A. Who in your life loves you because of you?

   B. What does it mean that God loves you because he is he? How can this truth give you great confidence?

   C. Discuss each element of God's love just mentioned: self-generated, uncaused, spontaneous, constant-level. How does each of these terms expand your concept of God's love?

2. Success signals God's love no more than struggles indicate the lack of it. The definitive, God-sanctioned gauge is not a good day or a bad break but the dying hours of his Son. Consider them often.

   A. Why does success not necessarily signal God's love? Why do struggles not indicate the lack of God's love?

   B. How do the dying hours of Jesus best show us God's love?

   C. How can you train yourself to think often of Christ's sacrifice? Name some practical steps you could take, starting today.

3. To abide in Christ's love is to make his love your home. Not a roadside park or hotel room you occasionally visit, but your preferred dwelling.

    A. What does it mean to you to "abide in Christ's love"?

    B. How can you make Christ's love your "preferred dwelling"?

    C. What tends to keep you from abiding in Christ's love? How can you overcome this obstacle?

4. God's love can't be legislated, but it can be chosen. Choose it, won't you? For the sake of your heart. For the sake of your home. For Christ's sake, and yours, choose it.

    A. Have you chosen God's love? Why or why not?

    B. How can choosing God's love improve your heart? How can it improve your home?

    C. How does it benefit Christ ("for Christ's sake") for you to choose God's love?

FILL YOUR CUP

1. Read Ephesians 3:16–19.

    A. For what did Paul pray in verse 16?

    B. What was the purpose of his prayer (v. 17)?

    C. For what else did Paul pray in verse 17?

    D. How does the apostle describe God's love in verses 18–19?

    E. What was the ultimate prayer of Paul in verse 19?

2. Read John 15:1–8.

    A. To what did Jesus compare himself in verse 1? To what did he compare his Father? What is significant about both images?

B. What divine activity does Jesus describe in verse 2?

C. What general principle of the Christian life is laid out in verse 4?

D. What promise is given in verse 5?

E. What warning is given in verse 6?

F. What additional promise is given in verse 7? On what does the promise depend?

G. What gives God glory, according to verse 8? How does this provide evidence of relationship to Christ?

DRINK DEEPLY

Perhaps one of the best ways to celebrate God's amazing love and grace is to share some of that love and grace with others. Who in your life—family member, coworker, neighbor, fellow church member—most needs encouragement right now? Think of some special, maybe even unusual way to show that person God's love. And remember this: *you* are not the center of attention! Maybe you could do something anonymously and leave the person wondering who could have been so thoughtful. Sometimes, secret displays of grace are the most fun!

FIFTEEN

Have You Heard the Clanging Door?

COME TO THE WELL

1. "Deny Jesus," Peter testified, "and he'll still love you." "Doubt Jesus," Thomas could add, "and the same is true."

   A. How could Jesus still love Peter after Peter had denied him?

   B. How could Jesus still love Thomas after Thomas had doubted him?

   C. If Jesus will still love us regardless of what we do, does it matter how we live? Explain.

2. Are you convinced that you have never lived a loveless day? Not one. Never unloved. Those times you deserted Christ? He loved you. You hid from him; he came looking for you.

   A. Answer the previous question.

   B. In what ways have you "deserted" Christ? What happened?

   C. How did Jesus come looking for you?

3. The jail door has never closed. God's love supply is never empty.

   A. How do we know that God's love supply is never empty?

   B. How have you most recently experienced God's love?

   C. How can you, today, show God's love to others?

4. The big news of the Bible is not that you love God but that God loves you; not that you can know God but that God already knows you! He tattooed your name on the palm of his hand. His thoughts of you outnumber the sand on the shore. You never leave his mind, escape his sight, flee his thoughts. He sees the worst of you and loves you still.

   A. How does it make you feel to realize that God knows you completely and still loves you utterly?

   B. How does it make you feel to know that God has tattooed your name on the palm of his hand?

   C. What do you imagine God is thinking about you at this moment?

FILL YOUR CUP

1. Read Romans 8:31–39.

   A. What question is asked in verse 31? What is the expected answer?

   B. What question is asked in verse 32? What is the expected answer?

   C. What questions are asked in verse 33? What are the expected answers?

   D. What questions are asked in verse 34? What is the apostle's response?

   E. What questions are asked in verse 35? What is the expected answer?

   F. What is the purpose of the Bible quotation in verse 36?

   G. How did the apostle see the troubles of life when viewed from his close connection to God (v. 37)?

H. What final conclusion does the apostle reach in verses 38–39?

2. Read 1 John 4:7–12.

A. What instruction is given in verse 7? What reason is given for the instruction? What general truth is expressed?

B. What bold statement is made in verse 8? What reason is given for this statement?

C. What major proof of the love of God is cited in verse 9?

D. What is true love, according to verse 10?

E. What instruction is given in verse 11? On what basis is this instruction given?

F. How can others see the invisible God and his love (v. 12)?

DRINK DEEPLY

To help remind you that, as Paul says, "If we are faithless, he will remain faithful, for he cannot disown himself" (2 Tim. 2:13 NIV), do a little exercise that might feel a bit uncomfortable. Sit down and make a catalog of the specific ways you believe you may have failed your Lord in the last year (let's not make this too depressing!). After you have finished your list, burn it—and remind yourself of the goodness of the Lord. Then give him joyful thanks and full-bodied praise for being who he is and acting as he does!

SIXTEEN

Fearlessly Facing Eternity

COME TO THE WELL

1. Payback. The evidence is in. The truth is out. And the policeman is standing at your door. No one likes the thought of judgment.

   A. What thoughts and feelings does judgment stir in you?

   B. If you were being paid back today, what kind of payment would you expect?

   C. Why do you think the Bible talks so much about judgment?

2. You will not be helped or hindered by the deeds of your family, church, or nation. You will be personally judged according to one question: "What did you do with Jesus?"

   A. Why will the deeds of your family, church, or nation not help you in the judgment to come?

   B. What have you done with Jesus?

   C. Why does everything hinge on your answer to this last question?

3. God views Christians the way he views Christ: sinless and perfect. Hence, Christians can view judgment the way Christ does: with confidence and hope.

A. How can God view Christians in the same way he views Christ?

B. Do you view judgment the same way Christ does? Explain.

C. What gives you the right to feel confidence and hope as you contemplate God's judgment? What have you done to deserve that right?

4. You need never fear God's judgment. Not today. Not on Judgment Day. Jesus, in the light of God's glory, is speaking on your behalf. "That's my friend," he says. And when he does, the door of heaven opens.

A. Do you think Jesus considers you his friend? Explain.

B. Do you expect the door of heaven to be opened for you on the day of judgment? Explain.

FILL YOUR CUP

1. Read 1 John 4:16–18.

A. What does it mean to "know" the love of God (v. 16)? How is it different to trust it or rely on it?

B. How is love made complete, or perfect, in us (v. 17)? What effect does this love have on us in the day of judgment? In what specific way does John expect followers of Jesus to be "like" him?

C. How do fear and love interact (v. 18)? If one fears divine judgment, what conclusion can be made?

2. Read Romans 2:5–11; 14:10–12; 2 Corinthians 5:9–10.

A. What "day" is in view in Romans 2:5?

B. What general principle of divine judgment is described in verse 6?

C. What group is described in verse 7? What can they expect to receive at the judgment (v. 10)?

D. What group is described in verses 8–9?

E. Why is it important to recognize the truth of verse 11?

F. What further details are given about this event in Romans 14:10–12?

G. What personal goal will serve us well when the day of judgment comes (2 Cor. 5:9)?

H. What additional details are given in 2 Corinthians 5:10?

DRINK DEEPLY

The Gospel of Matthew presents some of the most extended biblical teaching on the final judgment to be found anywhere in Scripture. In your quiet time some day, read Matthew 24:36–25:46. Put yourself into each of the varied scenes that Jesus describes. Where do you think you fit?

When you're ready for another study, take a close look at the little book of 1 Thessalonians. Each chapter of this book ends with a reference to the second coming of Christ. List the various things you learn about the return of Christ, take a whole day to meditate on each of these things, and then take a personal inventory to see how your study *has been* and *is* changing the way you live.

SEVENTEEN

If God Wrote You a Letter

COME TO THE WELL

1. Were no one to tell them, they would carry the box to their dirt-floored home, place it in a prime location, and admire it, display it, but never open it. Don't we do the same with Christ? Aren't we prone to keep him at arm's length?

   A. How do we tend to keep Christ at arm's length?

   B. Why do you think we tend to keep Christ at arm's length?

   C. What can you do today to personally experience the gift of Christ?

2. Through what faucets has God poured his love into your life? A faithful church? A prayerful spouse? Time-tested traditions? A girlfriend in college or a grandma from childhood?

   A. Answer the previous question.

   B. Why do you think God uses so many "faucets" to pour out his love?

   C. How can you be a "faucet" to pour out God's love on others?

3. The treasure is the Giver himself. On my list of things I wish I had learned earlier, this truth hovers near the top.

   A. Why is it so easy for our hearts to be captured by the gifts of God rather than by God himself?

B. What about God do you value the most? Why?

C. How can you train yourself to want the Giver more than his gifts?

4. Max lists four things that can help us drink from the bottomless well of Christ (these are also the four main divisions of the book): accept his work; rely on his energy; trust his lordship; receive his love.

A. In what ways have you accepted the work of God on your behalf? In what ways do you struggle to accept his work?

B. How have you learned to rely on God's energy? How do you still tend to rely on your own strength?

C. In what areas of life do you find it easiest to trust God's lordship? In what areas of life is this still a struggle?

D. How have you learned to receive God's love? When do you sometimes have a problem receiving God's love?

FILL YOUR CUP

1. Read Jeremiah 2:12–13.

A. How do you know that the statement about to be made in Jeremiah 2:13 is of enormous significance?

B. What two sins had the people of Jeremiah's time committed? What exchange had they made? What was so foolish about this exchange? How do we often make the same exchange? Why do you think we make it?

2. Read Isaiah 55:1–3.

A. Who is addressed in verse 1? What invitation is given?

B. What question is asked in verse 2? What answer could be given? What promise is made?

    C. What ultimate benefit is offered in verse 3? Have you accepted this benefit? Explain.

  3. Read John 7:37–39.

    A. What claim about himself is Jesus making in verse 37?

    B. What benefit does he promise to his listeners (v. 39)?

    C. What do his listeners have to do to enjoy this benefit (v. 38)?

DRINK DEEPLY

If you could write a letter to God that could be delivered this very day, what would you say in that letter? Take some time to write that letter—of thanks, of praise, of petition, or whatever you would like to say in such a special note—and then offer it to God. Keep the letter in a safe and special place and revisit it later, especially on dark and difficult days, so you can say along with the psalmist, "I am still confident of this: I will see the goodness of the LORD in the land of the living" (Ps. 27:13 NIV).

Notes

CHAPTER 2: SIN VACCINATION

1. I. D. E. Thomas, comp., *The Golden Treasury of Puritan Quotations* (Chicago: Moody Press, 1975), 266, quoted in Bruce A. Demarest, *The Cross and Salvation: The Doctrine of Salvation* (Wheaton, IL: Crossway Books, 1997), 29.

2. "Secrets of the Dead: Mystery of the Black Death," Public Broadcasting Service, http://www.pbs.org/wnet/secrets/case_plague/index.html and http://www.pbs.org/wnet/secrets/case_plague/clues.html.

CHAPTER 3: WHEN GRACE GOES DEEP

1. Charles Swindoll, *The Tale of the Tardy Oxcart and 1,501 Other Stories* (Nashville: Word Publishing, 1998), 250.

2. Ron Lee Davis with James D. Denny, *Mistreated* (Portland, OR: Multnomah Press, 1989), 147–48.

CHAPTER 4: WHEN DEATH BECOMES BIRTH

1. Rick Reilly, "Extreme Measures," *Sports Illustrated*, http://sportsillustrated .cnn.com./inside_game /rick_reilly/news/2003/05/20/life_of_reilly0519/3; Shane Burrows, "Cheating Death in Bluejohn Canyon," http://www .climb-utah.com/Roost/bluejohn2.htm; "Climber Describes Amputation Ordeal," CBS News, http://www.cbsnews.com/stories/2003/05/02/national/ main551979.shtml; "A Rational Choice," ABC News, http://abcnews. go.com/sections/GMA/US/GMA030506Climber_amputate.html.

2. "Climber Recounts Canyon Ordeal," http://www.msnbc.com/news/ 908232.asp.

3. Paul Aurandt, *Destiny and 102 Other Real Life Mysteries* (New York: Bantam Books, 1983), 28.

4. F. W. Boreham, *Life Verses: The Bible's Impact on Famous Lives* (Grand Rapids: Kregel Publications, 1994), 1:118.

CHAPTER 5: WITH HEART HEADED HOME

1. "Corridors of Agony," *Time*, 27 January 1992, quoted in Maxie Dunnam, *This Is Christianity* (Nashville: Abingdon Press, 1994), 133–34.

CHAPTER 7: WAITING FOR POWER

1. Brother Lawrence, *The Practice of the Presence of God* (Old Tappan, NJ: Revell, 1958), 9.

2. William Barclay, *The Acts of the Apostles* (Philadelphia: Westminster Press, 1976), 15.

CHAPTER 8: GOD'S BODY GLOVE

1. C. S. Lewis, *Mere Christianity* (New York: Macmillan Publishing Co., 1952), 167.

CHAPTER 9: IT'S NOT UP TO YOU

1. William C. Frey, *The Dance of Hope: Finding Ourselves in the Rhythm of God's Great Story* (Colorado Springs, CO: WaterBrook Press, 2003), 174.

CHAPTER 10: IN GOD WE (NEARLY) TRUST

1. Harold S. Kushner, *When Bad Things Happen to Good People* (New York: Avon Books, 1983), 42–43.

2. Margaret Clarkson, *Grace Grows Best in Winter: Help for Those Who Must Suffer* (Grand Rapids: W. B. Eerdmans, 1984), 40–41.

3. John Oxenham, *Bees in Amber: A Little Book of Thoughtful Verse*, The Project Gutenberg, http://www.gutenberg.net/etext06/8bees10.txt.

CHAPTER 11: WORRY? YOU DON'T HAVE TO

1. "Biosphere 2 Today, A New Dynamic for Ecosystem Study and Education," http://www.accessexcellence.org/LC/ST/st4bg.html.

2. Bob Russell with Rusty Russell, *Jesus, Lord of Your Personality: Four Powerful Principles for Change* (West Monroe: LA: Howard Publishing, 2002), 41.

3. R. G. V. Tasker, ed., *Tyndale New Testament Commentaries: The Epistle of Paul to the Philippians* (Grand Rapids: W. B. Eerdmans, 1976), 169.

CHAPTER 12: ANGELS WATCHING OVER YOU

1. Rick Reilly, "The Play of the Year," *Sports Illustrated*, 18 November 2002.

2. Francis Thompson, *The Kingdom of God*, quoted in Herbert Lockyer Jr., *All the Angels in the Bible* (Peabody, MA: Hendrickson Publishers, 1995), xv.

3. John Milton, *Paradise Lost*, bk. 4, lines 678–79.

4. Billy Graham, *Angels: God's Secret Agents* (Garden City, NY: Doubleday, 1975), 24.

CHAPTER 14: GOING DEEP

1. Gary Smith, "The Rapture of the Deep," *Sports Illustrated*, 16 June 2003, 62–78.

2. David Brainerd, quoted in Cynthia Heald, "Becoming a Friend of God," *Discipleship Journal*, no. 54 (1989): 22.

3. Craig Childs, *The Secret Knowledge of Water: Discovering the Essence of the American Desert* (Boston: Little, Brown and Company, 2000), 61–62.

CHAPTER 15: HAVE YOU HEARD THE CLANGING DOOR?

1. Patrick McGilligan, *Alfred Hitchcock: A Life in Darkness and Light* (New York: HarperCollins, 2003), 7–8. There are many variations to this story, and some believe it may be apocryphal.

CHAPTER 16: FEARLESSLY FACING ETERNITY

1. "Fear," sample illustrations, http://www.preachingplus.com.

2. H. A. Guy, *The New Testament Doctrine of the Last Things* (New York: Oxford University Press, 1948), 173, quoted in Frank Stagg, *New Testament Theology* (Nashville: Broadman Press, 1962), 305.

CHAPTER 17: IF GOD WROTE YOU A LETTER

1. Spiros Zodhiates et al., *A Treasury of Bible Illustrations* (Chattanooga, TN: AMG Publishers, 1995), 135.

2. Isa. 55:1; Isa. 51:12; 1 Cor. 6:20; Col. 2:10; Isa. 62:4–5; Heb. 13:5.

3. Amos 5:12; 2 Cor. 12:9; Isa. 38:17; Mic. 7:19; 1 Cor. 6:11; Isa. 44:22.

4. 1 Cor. 15:54; Col. 2:15; Heb. 2:14; Rev. 14:13; Phil. 3:20; Matt. 25:34; Rev. 21:4.

5. Luke 10:41; Prov. 3:5; 2 Pet. 2:9; Rom. 8:26; Col. 1:11; Rom. 8:32; Judg. 5:21; 2 Cor. 4:1; Isa. 41:10.

6. Isa. 26:4; 1 Pet. 2:25; Isa. 43:2.

7. Matt. 6:34; Ps. 121:4–5; Ps. 34:7; Ps. 31:20; Deut. 31:6; Ps. 37:23–24; Ps. 32:8.

8. Matt. 24:6; John 16:33; Phil. 4:6; Ps. 5:12.

9. Gen. 41:52; Isa. 61:3; Isa. 57:15; Ps. 30:5; Rom. 8:31.

10. Deut. 32:10 MSG; Zeph. 3:17; Ps. 139:17–18; Rom. 8:38.

11. Isa. 49:14–15; 1 Pet. 1:19; John 10:28; Isa. 49:16; John 15:15; Matt. 10:30–31.

12. Ps. 55:22; Ps. 103:13–14; 1 Pet. 5:7.

13. Phil. 4:5; Matt. 11:28; Ps. 149:4; Heb. 10:23; Rev. 22:17.

ONE VOICE ONE GOAL TO FIGHT GLOBAL AIDS & POVERTY

www.theonecampaign.org

There is a plague of biblical proportions taking place in Africa right now, but we can beat this crisis, if we each do our part. Step ONE is signing the ONE petition, to join the ONE Campaign.

The ONE Campaign is a new effort to rally Americans—ONE by ONE—to fight global AIDS and extreme poverty. We are engaging Americans everywhere we gather—in churches and synagogues, on the internet and college campuses, at community meetings and concerts. To learn more about *The ONE Campaign*, go to ***www.theonecampaign.org*** and sign the online petition.

> "...Babies need hugs. Children need good-night tucks. AIDS orphans need homes. Stressed-out executives need hope. God has work to do. *And he uses our hands to do it.*"
>
> —Max Lucado, *Come Thirsty*

ONE Voice can make a difference. Let God work through you; join the ONE Campaign now!

This campaign is brought to you by

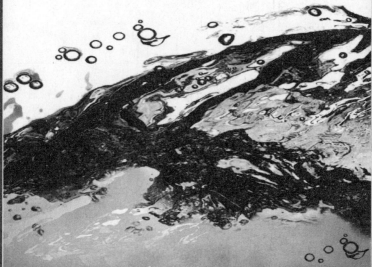

The Chronicles of the Cross Series

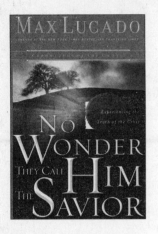

No Wonder they Call Him the Savior

In this compelling quest for the Messiah, best-selling author Max Lucado invites you to meet the blue-collar Jew whose claim altered a world and whose promise has never been equaled. You will come to know Jesus the Christ in a brand-new way as Lucado brings you full circle to the foot of the cross and the man who sacrificed his life on it. **ISBN 0-8499-1714-6**

And the Angels Were Silent

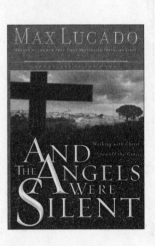

As Jesus entered His final days and faced Golgotha, He acted with loving purpose and deliberate intent. Each step was calculated. Every act premeditated.

Knowing He had just one week with His disciples, what did Jesus tell them? Where did He go? What did He do? What really mattered in those final hours? *And the Angels Were Silent* allows you to enter the holy week and take an intimate look at our Savior's last week. **ISBN 0-8499-1815-4**

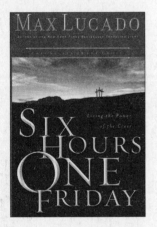

Six Hours One Friday

God promises to be with you, and He has provided you with three anchor points to help you ride out *any* storm. Each anchor point was planted firmly in bedrock two thousand years ago by a carpenter who claimed to be the Christ. It was all done during six hours one Friday. They were the most critical hours in history. Travel back to the foot of the cross and learn how to live in the power of the cross.

ISBN 0-8499-1816-2

W Publishing Group™
www.wpublishinggroup.com

Also from Max Lucado

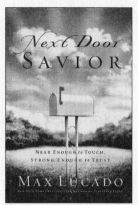

Available in Spanish editions

NEXT DOOR SAVIOR

The universe's Commander in Chief knows your name. He has walked your streets. Endowed with sleepless attention and endless devotion, he listens. The fact that we can't imagine how he hears a million requests as if they were only one doesn't mean he can't or doesn't. For He can and does. There is no person he won't touch. No place he won't go to find you. For even though he is in heaven, he never left the neighborhood. He is near enough to touch. Strong enough to trust. A next door Savior.

A LOVE WORTH GIVING

Finding it hard to love? Someone in your world is hard to forgive? Is patience an endangered species? Kindness a forgotten virtue? If so, you may have forgotten an essential first step. Living loved. God loves you. Personally. Powerfully. Passionately. Others have promised and failed. But God has promised and succeeded. He loves you with an unfailing love. And his love—if you let it—can fill you and leave you with a love worth giving.

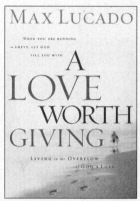

Available in Large Print and Spanish editions

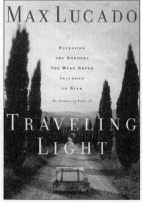

Available in Large Print and Spanish editions

TRAVELING LIGHT

No wonder we get so weary—we're worn out from carrying excess spiritual baggage. Wouldn't it be nice to lose some of those bags? That's the invitation of Max Lucado. With the twenty-third Psalm as our guide, we learn to release some of the burdens we were never intended to bear. Learn to lighten your load, as Max Lucado embraces what it really means to say, "The Lord is my Shepherd."

W PUBLISHING GROUP™

www.wpublishinggroup.com

Also from Max Lucado

HE CHOSE THE NAILS

Christ's sacrifice has defined the very essence of mankind's faith for the past 2000 years. Now Max Lucado invites you to examine the cross, contemplate its purpose, and celebrate its significance. With his warm, caring style, Max examines the symbols surrounding Christ's crucifixion, revealing the claims of the cross and asserting that if they are true, then Christianity itself is true. The supporting evidence either makes the cross the single biggest hoax of all time, or the hope of all humanity.

Available in Large Print and Spanish editions

HE DID THIS JUST FOR YOU

Building on stories and illustrations from the book *He Chose the Nails* by Max Lucado, *He Did This Just for You* is a 64-page evangelistic book that leads the readers through God's plan of salvation and offers an invitation to accept Christ. It's the perfect way to introduce the gospel to friends and acquaintances through Max Lucado's warm and easy to understand writing style. Experience God's Grace and plan of salvation for the first time or use this booklet to share the message of hope with someone you know.

Available in Spanish editions

AN ANGEL'S STORY

Was the birth of Jesus a quietly profound event? Or could it have included heavenly battles, angel armies, and a scheming Satan? Come along as Max Lucado takes us on a journey into his imagination—pulling back the curtain as we see what might have taken place in *An Angel's Story* (previously titled *Cosmic Christmas*).

W PUBLISHING GROUP™
www.wpublishinggroup.com